Fostering Civility on Campus

Judy Rookstool

Community College Press®
a division of the American Association of Community Colleges
Washington, DC

The American Association of Community Colleges (AACC) is the primary advocacy organization for the nation's community colleges. The association represents more than 1,100 two-year, associate degree–granting institutions and more than 11 million students. AACC promotes community colleges through six strategic action areas: national and international recognition and advocacy, learning and accountability, leadership development, economic and workforce development, connectedness across AACC membership, and international and intercultural education. Information about AACC and community colleges may be found at www.aacc.nche.edu.

Design: Grace Design, LLC
Editors: Deanna D'Errico
Printer: Kirby Lithographic

Community College Press
American Association of Community Colleges
One Dupont Circle, NW
Suite 410
Washington, DC 20036

Printed in the United States of America.

Library of Congress Cataloging-in-Publication Data

Rookstool, Judy.
    Fostering civility on campus / Judy Rookstool.
        p. cm.
    "Offers a definition of civility and common-sense approaches that instructors and administrators can use to foster and maintain a civil environment in the classroom and on campus"—Provided by publisher.
    Includes bibliographical references and index.
    ISBN 978-0-87117-379-9
    1. Moral education—United States. 2. Civics—Study and teaching (Higher)—United States. 3. Classroom environment—United States. I. Title.

LC311.R59 2007
370.11'4—dc22

2007009657

Contents

Preface

Because there is so much discussion decrying incivility and the increase of rudeness in society, I wanted to write a book from a positive stance in which civility becomes a means to building community on a college campus. And because I believe that civility is embedded in ethics and in one's participation as a citizen, as well as in human communication, this book draws upon a variety of fields to compile a notion of civility for the community college classroom.

Civility is a civic virtue commonly associated with politeness, good manners, and rectitude, but it is also an ethical principal that underlies respect for individual people and thus is a foundation of the civil state. Civility is not a prescription for behavior but a sense of the ethical underpinnings in social relations and mutual respect in discourse. Civility can be an emotionally loaded word, conjuring up images of too much silverware on the table; however, civility is a truly democratic word, sharing roots with *civil*, *civic*, and *civilized*.

My interest in civility and etiquette began when I was a child and my aunt and I had tea parties—planned in order to teach me manners. Later I observed that etiquette could be used in a harmful, exclusionary way to exhibit "superior" knowledge. (Etiquette was used, beginning early in the last century, to accentuate classes of Americans within society. In fact the proliferation of types of forks and their placement on the table was, in part, about acquisition of arcane, exclusionary knowledge as much as acquisition of silverware. Etiquette still may be used to cloak with false sweetness the cudgel of discrimination.) I wanted to understand the distinctions between etiquette, which is a codified set of manners, and civility, which is the underlying respect for "other."

A portion of this book addresses civility within the context of civil discourse and relates it to historical theory of civic virtue and civil society. However, the *praxis* has equal importance, and so there are implications and strategies for the classroom and the campus to encourage civil discourse, civility, and a strong learning environment.

Ideally, fostering a civil environment most conducive to student learning and future citizenship is the responsibility of everyone on campus. A college's teachers, student support services, and campus facilities all offer students opportunities for construction of knowledge (content) and development of skills essential for social interaction (process) as citizens in the community.

Understanding the Concept of Civility

A Concern Both Ancient and Modern

Decrying a lack of civility is not new. In 399 B.C., Aristotle reportedly said, "Children today love luxury too much. They have detestable manners, flout authority, and have no respect for their elders. They no longer rise when their parents and teachers enter the room. What kind of awful creatures will they be when they grow up?" The most recent cycle of concern seemed to begin in the late 1990s with a flurry of media attention. In 1996, the author of "The American Uncivil Wars," an article in *U.S. News & World Report*, reported that 89% of Americans thought incivility was a problem, and 78% thought it had gotten worse in the previous 10 years—a shift represented by an increase in a torrent of complaints in the popular press and media talk shows about how rude Americans have become (Marks, 1996).

That same year, civility was a topic of discussion at the newly formed Penn National Commission on Society, Culture and Community and, in March 1998, was the subject of a major national conference, "Reassessing Civility," at Johns Hopkins University. Also in 1998, the mayor of New York initiated civility classes for municipal employees, and, in 1999, Louisiana passed a law requiring courtesy of school children. Around this time also, secondary educators began addressing incivility in the schools as an issue of "character education."

Since then, interest in the topic has produced numerous other articles and meetings, as well as books. For example, P. M. Forni, co-founder of the Johns Hopkins Civility Project, wrote *Choosing Civility: Twenty-five Rules of Considerate Conduct* (2002), in which he urged people—in the classroom and in the larger society—toward "thoughtful behavior and common decency." Forni enumerated these basic rules to provide a "handbook for the practical use of civility" (2002, p. xi), with an emphasis on mutual respect and consideration for others. This sense of mutual consideration related to moral authority (and also humor) is also found in the practical advice on ethics of Randy Cohen in *The Good, The Bad, and the Difference* (2002). Cohen, author of "The Ethicist" column for the *New York Times Magazine*, explicated the ethics of everyday behavior in public and private life (including a chapter on school life). He said, "Just as individual ethics can only be understood in relation to the society within which it is practiced, it is also true that individual ethical behavior is far more likely to flourish within a just society" and suggested that "to lead an ethical life one must work to build a just society" (2002, p. 9).

I believe, as Forni and Cohen clearly do, that the concept of civility is embedded in ethics and in one's participation as a citizen, as well as in human communication. In writing this book, therefore, I have drawn from a variety of fields to help college instructors and administrators reach a common understanding of what civility means and how to apply that understanding at the classroom level. To that end, in this chapter I offer a working definition of civility and a summary of the theory that informs it.

The Meaning of Civility

Most people associate civility with etiquette or manners. But civility is a multifaceted concept with many shades of meaning. And although the concepts of etiquette and manners are integral to the definition of the word, even they have distinctly different meanings. Etiquette is a system of codified rules established by a particular society to govern social conduct, whereas manners is a broader concept. As Amy Vanderbilt stated, "etiquette has to do with when you wear white gloves and how you unfold your napkin in your lap; real manners are being thoughtful toward others" (cited in Kingwell, 1995, p. 215).

To discover how richly nuanced the term *civility* is, one need only to look it up in the *Oxford English Dictionary* (2nd edition): Its definition occupies nearly half a page. Here is a brief excerpt, which supplies its most common meanings succinctly:

> 1) connected with citizenship, a community of citizens collectively;
> 2) behavior proper to the intercourse of civilized people; 3) ordinary
> courtesy or politeness, as opposed to rudeness of behavior; 4)
> decent respect, consideration; 5) an act or expression of politeness;
> 6) decency, seemliness.

What is interesting to note in this definition is that whereas civility does denote courtesy, politeness, respect, consideration, and decency—all of which relate to etiquette and manners—the primary meanings relate to citizenship and civil discourse. These are the meanings that this book will be most concerned with, because, as I hope to demonstrate, they are the aspects of civility that are of central importance for engendering civil conduct in the classroom. To understand how citizenship and civil discourse came to be so integral to the concept, it is important to understand how the ethical principles civility is founded on have been debated through the ages. In the following summary, I trace the ethical components of civility, selecting from political and moral philosophy, as well as from communication theory.

The Ethical Underpinnings of Civility

With roots in both Greek and Enlightenment philosophy, civility finds a home in many modern philosophical theories. Philosopher James Rachels (1999) described morality as the effort to guide one's conduct by reason while giving weight to the interests of each individual who will be affected by one's conduct. Individuals should do what there are the best reasons for doing, but Western philosophers have disagreed about how to decide among the reasons.

The concept of *divine command*, which defined morality as whatever is commanded by a god or gods, predominated in Western thought until the 1700s, although the connection between religion and morality was questioned as early as Socrates' time. Later, natural law, a concept derived from the Greeks, held that everything has a purpose and that the way things are is the way they ought to be. Natural law posited that people are social creatures who care for others, and those who do not are somehow defective. Thus, civility was expected of (free) citizens in society.

Natural law endured into the Middle Ages, until it was surpassed by the fascination with science and reason during the Enlightenment. At this time moral philosophers took a variety of roads. Philosopher Thomas Hobbes held that all intentional human action is motivated by self-interest and that individuals cannot help but act to secure their own good. From this point of view, civility is practiced with an expectation that civility will be returned in kind and realized as peaceful life achieved; conversely, incivility may lead to further incivility.

According to Rachels (1999), *social contract theory* evolved as a practical solution to the problem that arises from self-interested action, a solution in the form of an agreement to establish a government to make social living possible. The social contract is most associated with Jean-Jacques Rousseau, who said agreement with the hypothetical social contract allows people to care for others simply because they are released from the fear of others. Rousseau also believed in the "voice of duty," which requires one to set aside self-centeredness in favor of the welfare of everyone equally (Rachels, 1999). The social contract provides the basis for the civil state understanding of civility.

For humanist philosopher Immanuel Kant, morality was a matter of following absolute rules with no exceptions and of relying ultimately on reason. Kant believed moral obligations to be categorical regardless of personal desires and possible only because humans possess reason. Kant's central philosophical concept was called the categorical imperative: "Act only according to that maxim by which you can at the same time will that it would become a universal law." That is, do only what you would want everybody to do. The practice of courtesy or civility, therefore, becomes the right thing to do.

Although many have criticized the categorical imperative, Kant's ideas have influenced much of Western philosophy, especially in various forms of *universalism*—concepts and issues that are said to transcend localizing boundaries. Equality and respect for all, for example, is an important part of democratic government and a central notion of public education. Universalism led to current *communication theory*, which is based on the idea that by being open to others, human beings can reach an understanding on questions of importance through their ability to reason and deliberate. Language and communication attain new prominence. Following this philosophical path, civility becomes part of the discussion to reach understanding.

Ethical subjectivism is based on the idea that there is no objective right or wrong, so that moral judgments are purely the expression of personal feelings. Nineteenth-century *utilitarianism* provided a radical new conception of morality: the principle of choosing from among alternatives that which has the best consequences for all concerned. Utilitarianism, in various forms, is resilient today, although it may be at odds with theories of individual rights and justice theory (Rachels, 1999).

Ethical relativity is the notion that, because different groups have different social practices and societies may have different moral codes, people cannot presume to evaluate the standards of others according to any absolute scale. This school of thought gained acceptance in the 1960s and persists in modified form. Because courtesy is exhibited in different ways in different societies, it is not possible, according to this belief, to evaluate such acts. The word *civility* may not translate literally across cultures, but the open-minded person examines courtesies and ritual acts for the underlying respect represented.

Virtue ethics, first conceived as Aristotle's questions about what constitutes living a good life, is related to civic virtue and the ethic of caring. It was first put forth in modern form by G. E. M. Anscombe in 1958 (see Rachels, 1999). Although the theory has not been fully developed by modern philosophers, virtue ethics defines what a virtue is, specifies virtuous character traits, and explains why ethics are important. In public schools, virtue ethics has taken the sometimes-controversial form of "character education," which defines character traits that should be fostered in students. Civility, within this realm of thought, is a virtue to be fostered in society by social institutions.

A relatively new idea in philosophy is the *ethic of caring* (see Gilligan, 1982; Noddings, 1984). Related to the idea of civic virtue, the ethic of caring has been applied to family and school and is, according to some, associated with feminism. Because many philosophers believed that women think differently than do men, the development of feminism has prompted the scholarly reconsideration of male-oriented concepts in philosophy and psychology, as well as in other disciplines. In *In a Different Voice*, Gilligan (1982) posited that women may relate moral questions to their surrounding relationships more than to universal moral concepts, but their morality is no less developed. Civility is an integral part of relationships that involve caring.

Civic Virtue and Civil State

When considering what binds society, the notion of *civic virtue* has been differentiated from *civil state* or *civil society* as questions arise about the appropriate stance for individuals with respect to their community or government. Civic virtue, with its foundation in ancient Greece, finds a modern incarnation in *communitarianism* (a theory that emphasizes the role of the community in defining and shaping individuals), communication theory, and virtue ethics. *Civil state*—also called *civil society*—theory derives from Thomas Aquinas, Kant, and the Scottish moralist philosophers and is consistent with *consequentialism*, the theory that valid moral judgments about any action must be based on the consequences of that action. The concept of civility has received renewed attention in the past several years by proponents of almost every political and ideological persuasion. This trend has led to a great deal of polarization among libertarians, communitarians, family value Republicans, neoliberals, justice theorists, and communication theorists, each of whom has a different definition of civil society and civility.

Civic Virtue

Aristotle (c. 325 BC) considered matters of character "an activity of the soul in conformity with virtue" (Rachels, 1999). Along with Socrates and Plato, Aristotle defined the traits of character that make one a good person, including virtues such as courage, self-control, generosity, and truthfulness. Within Greek and Roman political philosophy, the city-state was the model of republican virtue. According to Aristotle, citizenship was fully defined only within the sphere of political activity, and the moral ideal was public virtue—a communal enterprise —so community constituted morality (Seligman, 1992). The very word *ethic*, the Greek root of which is *ethikos*, means an ethos rooted in community and transmitted through custom (Eberly, 1998). With the spread of monotheism, the consideration of virtues gave way to Divine Law that emphasized righteous life as obedience to divine commandments.

Recently, there have been proponents of a return to ethics based in virtue. For example, Yale law professor Stephen L. Carter (1998) combined the idea of virtue founded in religion with the development of community: "We should make sacrifices for others not simply because doing so makes social life easier, but as a signal of respect for our fellow citizens, marking them as full equals, both before the law and before God" (p. 11). Civic virtue, however, is not granted by the state, and although for some proponents of civic virtue it is defined by a deity, for most it is the consequence of mutually and communally understood traits of virtue. There is no right to civility; it develops from collective conscience (Seligman, 1992).

Don Eberly described a whole movement that has arisen to recover societal virtue, which he defined as having several related objectives:

> It reflects a search for new citizenship that is less self-centered, more civil, and civically engaged. It is an attempt to draw Americans together at a time of isolation and fragmentation, to restore community institutions, to transcend political differences in order to become neighbors again, to recover the spirit of volunteerism, and more. (1998, p. 5)

Eberly suggested a variety of strategies for renewing the culture, including development of character education, more reliance on volunteerism, and re-moralizing culture. Considered to be conservative politically, Eberly was concerned that "the state creeps in where moral consensus retreats," and that in a "nonstatist society, culture must play the lead role in establishing boundaries" (1998, p. 13). Although it is unclear *which* culture he meant, he was very direct in asserting as the basis of moral consensus a return to religion.

Nannerl Keohane, past president of Duke University and Wellesley College, has asserted that principles of civic virtue and ethics have substantial implications for higher education. Keohane defined the components of civic virtue suitable for an educational setting, which include "an understanding of the interconnectedness of human beings," subordination of selfish impulses to the needs of others, tolerance for people whose ways are different, and "a readiness to collaborate with others in order to achieve desirable goals" (1996, p. 2). Keohane said that we can no longer assume that students are taught such principles; however, "colleges and universities are uniquely well-placed to train young people in the rudiments of civic virtue." This is because campuses are "concentrated human communities" with many of the challenges and opportunities present in the world that "offer daily practical experience in the consequences of ethical and unethical behavior" (1996, p. 2). Although community colleges do not always foster the close association of on-campus living, the interaction found in classes and co-curricular activities have some of the same challenges to and opportunities for the development of ethical behavior. Keohane also said that a civic virtue model can provide a foundation for acquiring other virtues and provides "a sturdy and supple framework for living in, and leading, a pluralist democracy" (1996, p. 6).

Communitarianism

Communitarianism has its roots in the concept of civic virtue; that is, that values are derived from the community, and individuals owe a strong responsibility to the community and to one another. It is a "group as family" concept where history and tradition forge the bonds. The communitarian agenda has been somewhat controversial, existing as it does in a society founded on individual rights. Amitai Etzioni (1993) developed what he called the platform of a communitarian society: "a new moral, social, and public order without Puritanism or oppression." Communitarians advocate a balancing of rights and responsibilities and what Etzioni calls a "shoring up of morality" (1993, p. 23). He stated, "The times call for an age of reconstruction in which we put a new emphasis on 'we,' on values we share, on the spirit of community" (1993, p. 25). He further developed the communitarian agenda in the context of family, schools, and politics, assuring readers that although community values can lead to excesses (e.g., neo-Nazism, banning books), the overarching values of the society will prevail.

Wlodzimierz Wesolowski speculated that college teachers resemble communitarians in that they accept some fundamental values, such as social democratic principles, and resolve conflicts pragmatically (see Hall, 1995). One criticism of communitarianism is that a community of commonalities can exclude those who do not share those commonalities. Etzioni has worked to keep the communitarian agenda democratic, but according to Benjamin Barber, former director of the Walt Whitman Center for Culture and Politics of Democracy at Rutgers University, "The communitarian thirst for the restoration of lost values and value communities encourages people to impose their own cultural values....In the resulting solidaristic community, insiders favor identity over equality" (1998, p. 70). Russell Hardin (1995) was even more cautious when he speculated that the same commonality implicit in communitarians has inspired, in its excesses, ethnic cleansing. From the communitarian perspective, civility is of great value as a civic virtue, but not if it does not extend beyond a particular community to all of society.

Communication Theory

The concept of civility is put into practice as individuals communicate with one another in discourse. The very act of communication, which is intended to reach understanding, creates change in both partners in dialogue. Hans-Georg Gadamer believed that truth is to be validated in language by a community of interpreters who always bring with them their personal history. "Language is the language of reason itself," he said (1988, p. 363). All reason functions within the traditions to which they belong, the key to which is language. This principle of communicative understanding resonates well with civility.

When communication is oriented toward reaching understanding, claims are accepted implicitly, without explicit questioning and validation. For Jürgen Habermas (1979), discourse among competent communicators always involves these claims. This key concept, which draws on a particular interpersonal relationship between the speaker and the listener, forms the basis of *communicative action*. According to communication theory, civility can be practiced only as a means of reaching mutual understanding

Civil State Theory

Until the 18th century, the concept of the civil state did not exist, and the terms *civilization* and *civility* were used interchangeably, because the civil state, or public realm, had not yet been differentiated from the private realm. During the Enlightenment, however, philosophers gave more consideration to what constituted the public versus the private sphere. Kant placed freedom and equality in the public sphere. He separated civil society from the state and separated the public collective will, including matters of right and duties, from the private realm of morality and ethics (Seligman, 1992, p. 43–44). According to Adam Seligman, it was David Hume who separated reason and morality and emphasized the concept of reciprocity, so the rules of justice no longer depended on morality and thus became civil matters. Seligman saw this shift as related to the development of a market economy and cited economic philosopher Adam Smith who said, "The ethical idea in the civil society tradition is a private one, realized within the hearts and minds and acts of exchange of individual social actors" (cited in Hall, 1995, p. 209).

Following the tradition of the Scottish moralists, Seligman said, "to provide a new foundation for reciprocity, mutuality, and cooperation" (cited in Hall, 1995, p. 203), philosophers influenced heavily the Anglo-American view of civil society, positing its foundation ethics as residing within the individual conscience. The North American view of civil society is largely the result of this notion, in which morality is seen as a private matter; the individual and his or her conscience define the moral order but also maintain the "communal locus of individual life" (cited in Hall, 1995, p. 206). So laws governing societal matters are determined by the civil society, but matters of morality and conscience remain private. For proponents of civil state theory, the discussion of citizenship and civility takes place among individuals within the public sphere of moral community but outside of the state.

Universalism

John Rawls (1972) defined the liberal universalist position. Drawing upon Kant, John Locke, and Rousseau, he proposed inviolable individual justice that cannot be overridden by the welfare of society as a whole. For Rawls, justice is linked to the Aristotelian concept of the good, and he delineated principles for individuals as "the natural duties." These include "the duty of helping another when he is in need, provided that one can do so without excessive risk or loss to oneself" and the duty not to harm or injure another, nor to cause unnecessary suffering (1972, p. 114). In later work, Rawls supported the idea of politeness (see Ryfe, 1998), perhaps as it relates to his notion of the "necessity of social interdependence" (Rawls, 1972, p. 434). Thus, within a framework of individual rights, an individual has responsibility to others as a member of the larger society.

Toward Citizenship and Civil Discourse

Although the philosophical strands of civic virtue and civil state have often separated intellectual stances on the development of citizenship, they continue to inform both everyday and scholarly discourse on participation as a citizen in this society.

Civil Conversation

University of Toronto philosopher Mark Kingwell (1995) examined what appear to be divergent tracks—civil state and civic virtue—selecting useful components of both to provide a new perspective. Kingwell posited that people need to address justice as a social interaction in a pluralistic society, with less weight given to norms and principles than to the conversation in which they are justified. For example, generating the definition of civility as a virtue has most of its importance in the interaction of the "the talkers who do the generating and justifying." Kingwell has argued that "the best route to vigorous public debate lies in this conversational virtue of civility" (1995, p. viii).

Civility, politeness, and manners each have a slightly different emphasis in social interaction for Kingwell:

> In the context of dialogic justice, *civility* is centrally allied (if not strictly identical) to linguistic *politeness*; when understood as an orientation proper to citizenship, civility's two sides are self-restraint and *tact*. And civility is usefully distinguished both from *manners* (the rule-governed aspects of politeness) and from *etiquette* (the study and codification of manners). (1995, p. 197)

Linguistic politeness is a part of civility, a stance taken in the larger context of citizenship in society. Kingwell acknowledged the difficulty of conversation in a pluralistic society and suggested that civil constraint is a rational choice to achieve desired ends. For him, civility is a practical notion. We temper our feelings "not because we think conversation in itself a nice and cultured thing." We practice civility "because that is the only way, short of open warfare, that we can get [some of] the things we want." For the disparate groups in an educational community, civility and civil discourse become pragmatic means of relating to one another. Civility and civil discussion then become a rational and practical choice.

Civility is essential for living in a multicultural society but becomes difficult when a variety of ethical concepts are present. Kingwell has reconceived the role of justice to include sensitivity to and toleration of varying moral concepts, because "civility is culturally determined, present in determinate forms in given societies and not others" (1995, p. 43). "In society we always operate under voluntary restraints, restraints associated with social role-taking, sensitivity to context, and the perceptions of the pragmatic goals given to a particular situation" (1995, p. 43). Under these circumstances, civility is a rational choice and an attempt to reach understanding, similar to the sense in which understanding is used in communication theory.

Civil Society

Barber has examined both the libertarian and communitarian agendas and found them unable to provide a place for what he calls "us" as ordinary people. He defined an alternative in "strong democratic civil society," which is "neither governmental nor strictly private yet shares the virtues of both" (1998, p. 44). Barber also laid claim to civility in his alternative "where political discourse is grounded in mutual respect and the search for common understanding even as it expresses differences and identity conflicts" (1998, p. 44). Barber's list of practical approaches to reestablishing civil society include, among others, civic education and community service. "Putting service in the context of civil society and treating it as a concomitant of education makes it a first step toward lifelong citizenship....It is recognized as a crucial component of a responsible academic curriculum that accepts schools as parts of their communities and treats students as prospective citizens whose education must include civic competence." (1998, pp. 106–107)

For Barber, restoring the civility of discourse is an important way to repair civil society. He said, "Civil talk is in the first instance public talk, but making talk public is not automatically to civilize it" (1998, p. 115). He gave the example of talk radio, which is not in the least bit civil. He would repair public talk—introducing what he calls "civil talk"—with the concepts of commonality, deliberation, inclusiveness, provisionality, listening, learning, lateral communication (among citizens), imagination, and empowerment. Barber has said that people need to moderate their voices so the voices of others can be heard, and to be open to learning, which "presumes that opinion is mutable and that viewpoints can be modified and can grow" (1998, p. 119). Barber has unfolded a perspective with selected elements from liberalism and communitarianism to form an alternative he calls "strong democratic civil society," which reasserts civility and civil discourse.

Mutual Respect

One way to define civil discourse is as a respectful exchange of ideas that entails reason and thought. The principles of civil discourse include information exchange in dialogue, regard for the interests and claims of others, and orientation toward mutual understanding. Kingwell posited a more confrontational definition. "Civility as I interpret it still allows ample room for giving offense and for making politically unpopular or even dangerous claims. But these must be claims that are offered as part of an ongoing dialogue of justification—that is, open to further assessment by interlocutors. They must be *claims*, in short, and not simply abuse or insult" (1995, p. 245).

Certainly, civility cannot be a superficial plea for everyone to get along. According to Eberly, "If mean-spirited public debate is unhealthy for democracy, so is a civility that is synonymous with fuzziness and fudging" (1998, p. 102). He said that an already cynical public cannot countenance civility as "the latest ploy" by politicians. Eberly set forth two "irreducible requirements" of civil public discussion:

1. Acknowledging that democracy is enriched by competing ideologies and political perspectives and that competition over ideas therefore must be conducted honestly and openly
2. Possessing a genuine respect for the rights and dignity of one's opponents as human beings (1998, p. 102)

Law cannot impose civility that is developed as a virtue based on respect for people, and the adoption of civility in civil discourse means restraint in the manner of conversation, not of its content. Nothing in civility should be a limit to free speech, unless free speech is defined as saying to everyone every-thing on one's mind at all times—no matter what. The suggestion of civility is posed to encourage dialogue that can continue over time based on listening, respect, and openness. This stance comes from within as a result of developing respect as a virtue.

In *A Short History of Rudeness: Manners, Morals, and Misbehavior in Modern America* (1999), Caldwell examined issues of race and gender with regard to civility. Referring to misunderstandings among groups "fated to interdependence yet mutually suspicious," Caldwell says, "Relations have been poisoned by the massed forces of an abusive political, social, and economic history, whose shadows never seem to dissipate even where the worst oppressions have abated or even evaporated (1999, p. 168)." Caldwell cited examples of incidents where actions taken by people in different groups can result in far different perceptions, hurt, offense, and more hurt. Of relations among races, Caldwell said, "If everyone could be brought to agree not only that our past history bears a burden of racial injustice, but that we inherit that burden in a pervasive syndrome of instinctive prejudices we could posit some simple rules for inter-racial etiquette" (1999, p. 171).

Caldwell suggested that citizens agree that some groups have reason to bristle at any remark that appears to presume social inferiority; however, even that discomfort is hard to define and hard to discuss. "Race is not lifestyle; any conflict arising from it raises troubling moral questions, and strikes a nerve in human relations," according to Caldwell (1999, p. 170). No less difficult is the dynamic of relations among and between men and women, gay and straight. "Whatever their relative importance as occasions of oppression, gender is clearly different from race in one respect: it presents a more universal problem" (1999, p. 172). An excess of politeness been used as a mask for many forms of prejudice, but such false politeness is unrelated to civility. Some conflate incivility with racism—and indeed the effect may be difficult to distinguish—but prejudice is related to oppression of a group whereas incivility is ignoring relationships in the larger society and occurs one person at a time.

> "Civility is linked to the Latin word *civitas*, which means 'city' and 'community.' Thus, civility implies a larger social concern. When we are civil we are members in good standing of a community. We are good neighbors and good citizens. Whether we look at the core of manners or civility we discern not only pleasant form but ethical substance as well."—
> Hudson Valley Community College (2007)

Implications of Civility Theory for Academic Leaders

In *Democracy and Education*, philosopher and educator John Dewey linked civility with learning and democracy:

> A democracy is more than a form of government; it is primarily a mode of associated living, of conjoint communicated experience. The extension in space of the number of individuals who participate in an interest so that each has to refer his own action to that of others, and to consider the action of others to give point and direction to his own, is equivalent to breaking down those barriers

of class, race, and national territory which keep men from perceiving the full import of their activity. (1916/1963, p. 87)

Because civility implies understanding differing views, thus the opportunity to broaden one's thinking and to learn, civility supports academic as well as democratic ideals. For academic leaders, understanding how civility functions in the classroom setting entails a consideration of these questions:

- What constitutes civil society and civil discourse?
- What are responsibilities of an individual in the shared public sphere?
- How and why does one person respect another?
- What part does ethics play for the individual within a community, including an academic community?
- What are the responsibilities of academic leaders in guiding civil discourse?

Many in academia believe that speech should not be restrained in any way, and there is resistance to what is referred to as politically correct language and, admittedly, some language becomes tortured in the effort to be sensitive. Some would pit the oppression in race and gender in society or on campus against free speech. Certainly some college mission statements reflect this ongoing argument. What is important is the respect that underlies civility and civil discourse. In the narrowly defined community of the college, educators, administrators, and students have the opportunity to discuss and resolve such issues and to model civility through their leadership and citizenship. Etzioni said:

Moral education is fostered through personal example, and above all through fostering the proper educational culture— from the corridors and cafeteria to the parking lot and sports. In effect, the whole school should be considered as a set of experiences generating situations in which young people learn the values either of civility, sharing, and responsibility to the common good or of cheating, cutthroat competition, and total self-absorption. (1993, p. 259)

Although Etzioni was referring to students younger than those in community college, advocating and reinforcing shared values can and should take place at the college level. Consider that a community college not only draws from the community for its students but returns to the community educated beings who possess skills and knowledge and a capacity to contribute to that community. If the classroom can be likened to a civil society and the traditional role of the instructor is as the sovereign, then the instructor is in a position to define and model civil discourse. The responsibility of the instructor goes beyond imparting content to fostering citizenship. The instructor models respect for learning and respect for participants in the learning process; the instructor encourages discussion that is mutually respectful and tolerant of other views.

There are obstacles, however, to providing what is called civic education. "The most significant obstacles to civic education on campus today are in our own practices and expectations," said Keohane (1996, p. 3). "Faculty and staff members, to whom students look as sources of authority and also as role models, are for a variety of reasons hesitant to confront moral dilemmas head-on, or to engage in what might seem to be a form of preaching or social engineering" (p. 3). Educators are hesitant to present ourselves as models of behavior and uncomfortable with providing moral advice. "At a time when even parents are reluctant to stand in loco parentis, it is hardly surprising that faculty and staff hesitate to do so" (p. 3). Faculty should, however, be attentive to lessons in their behavior that may be learned by students and accept the reality that they are, in fact, role models for students. However, students who may see themselves as consumers of education can now select from among a variety of educational venues, including electronic training, and may rely less on traditional instructors as role models.

Although there seems little disagreement about whether courtesy and civility may be a good thing in the classroom, there may be disagreement about how civility may be applied in the classroom and how much civility is a good thing (as balanced with individual rights and free speech). Civility must never be used to stifle or control classroom discourse, but it can set the terms of respect for civil discourse. P. M. Forni, who founded the Hopkins Civility Project in 1997, stated, "I think there is educational value in behaving as persons of integrity, compassion, and empathy not because we are compelled by a written statement, but because we believe that is the right thing to do, and it's freely chosen" (cited in Dechter, 2007).

Based on data gathered in the San José City College Campus Climate Study (1998) and information obtained in student group interviews, it appears that students can identify the presence or absence of courtesy and civility and, for the most part, believe it to be valuable. Based on these interviews, informal conversations among colleagues (including faculty and staff), and selected literature, I describe more specifically in the next two chapters reasons for fostering civility in the classroom and some strategies for doing so.

CHAPTER TWO

Why Civility in the Classroom Matters

Although explication of theory establishes the underpinnings of civility, it is *praxis* (from Greek, meaning "to do") that provides the means to implement the concept. I have used the theory in Chapter 1 to inform the way in which the two strands of civility—citizenship (civic virtue/civil state) and civil discourse—are integral to the classroom.

Because Diversity Matters

As prominent a topic of public discussion as civility is that of diversity. The fact is that our society and, therefore, our communities and education system, are becoming increasingly more diverse. The issue of diversity has been at the forefront of attention in the United States partly because of ongoing and renewed turmoil at home and abroad—turmoil rooted in cultural differences—and partly because embracing diversity is key to succeeding in a global economy.

Community colleges play a prominent and unique role in promoting cultural sensitivity and understanding:

- Community colleges educate nearly half of all U.S. undergraduates: 46% (National Center for Education Statistics [NCES], 2004).
- Nearly one third of community college students are from ethnic or racial groups other than White (NCES, 2004).
- By virtue of their shared mission, community colleges are committed to serving not only individual students but also the communities in which they live.

As community colleges assume greater and greater importance in teaching increasingly diverse students, they are called upon to furnish effective, meaningful knowledge and useful life skills. For that task, colleges need to focus on a common purpose: the education of students. But that education cannot take place if differences among students or between students and faculty are not addressed. "The campus is one of the few places in America today where people have easy opportunities to learn from one another the ethical practices of different cultures, and the imperative importance of living more humanely together and caring for one another" (Keohane, 1996, p. 4).

Although we function within our cultural traditions, in order to understand one another we must also be open to the traditions of others. Gadamer wrote:

> Just as we cannot continually misunderstand the use of a word without its affecting the meaning of the whole, so we cannot hold blindly to our own fore-meaning of the thing if we would understand the meaning of another. Of course, this does not mean that when we listen to someone or read a book we must forget all our fore-meaning concerning the context, and all our own ideas. All that is asked is that we remain open to the meaning of the other person or text. (1988, p. 238)

Gadamer suggested that openness leads to a "fusion of horizons," during which one's self changes, and the new self incorporates the learning of another, a concept that, in the classroom setting, has implications for the quality of learning. Intercultural openness fosters shared knowledge, which is key to civil discourse (Habermas, 1979). When people are engaged in debate, shared knowledge forms the basis of dialogue that is aimed at reaching agreement while also taking into account the ideas of others.

Openness is not the same as tolerance. Tolerance, at the bare minimum, may mean hearing without necessarily being open to what one hears. According to Judith Rodin, former president of the University of Pennsylvania and former chair of the Penn National Commission on Society, Culture and Community, "As the complexities and realities of issues are exposed, a spectrum of positions should emerge, not merely a rigid polarization that stereotypically assigns everyone to one extreme or the other" (1998, p. 11). Rodin asserted that those engaged in public discourse, especially in the classroom, must remain open to other viewpoints rather than merely defending their own.

Kingwell underscored the need for openness and tolerance in discussion, saying "Civility contributes to smooth social interaction, makes for tolerance of diversity, and conditions a regard for the claims and interests of others. It is a decentering strategy that deflects concerns from my beliefs and claims to take account of those held by persons with whom I am interacting" (1995, p. 219). By practicing civil conduct and relying on civility in discussion, one is less immersed in one's own beliefs and more open to the ideas of another. Sissa (1998) also alluded to civility as a facilitator of social interaction. Being at ease with someone who is different from oneself is not just about manners; it is a measure of competence in a diversity of cultures. So-called diversity competence is widely cited as a crucial skill for thriving in a global economy.

The laws that govern a democratic society are usually consensual and, in the public sphere, are separate from moral matters such as ethics and religion. Pagden (1998) suggested that in a multicultural society, we limit some actions of different cultures, and each culture becomes different as a result. For example, he cited the exemption of Sikhs from most helmet laws because their religion requires them to wrap their heads with cloth. According to Pagden, although there is increasing reliance on law as a remedy for individual conflict, at the beginning of the 21st century, what will mediate among cultures will not be law but civility.

Because Citizenship Matters

Schools are socially embedded institutions. Sociologist Émile Durkheim asserted that society is a system of interconnected parts and that schools are both part of the system and mechanisms for maintaining and improving society. Education, which includes the teaching of norms and values such as civility, is the means by which society recreates itself. In Durkheim's view, civility includes the narrow concept of behavior and manners as well as the broader concept of civic responsibility, which entails accountability of an individual to the society at large (cited in McDill, 1998). Only the state can cut across parochial society to conduct public education to ensure social stability. The community college, as an institution formed to both draw upon and contribute to the community, is essential in the development of community values among its citizens.

Civility is a cornerstone of deliberative democracy and is the mechanism for civil discourse. Education institutions serve social purposes in that they teach the virtues of living in a democratic society. However, political philosophers and educators are often at odds over what constitutes civic education. Liberals who cite 19th-century British philosopher John Stuart Mill insist that civic education cannot be conducted to stifle division of opinion. But even strict justice theorist John Rawls emphasized teaching "toleration and mutual respect" and a sense of "fairness and civility as basic political virtues" (cited in Gutmann, 1995). According to Amy Gutmann, president of the University of Pennsylvania, who has written about issues of societal justice, public school is a means of establishing civility: "Liberal democratic governments can try to persuade close-minded individuals to respect reasonable opposition, but the realm of public schooling is a democratic government's single most powerful and legitimate means of teaching respect for reasonable public disagreement" (1987, p. 579).

Without a focus on the democratic common good, public discussion is more a matter of expression than deliberation. According to historian Robert Wiebe of Northwestern University, democracy requires a rational structure, and "rules in a genuine democracy must be negotiated among all participants. If there is such a thing as the common good, it needs to emerge out of the democratic process itself" but "democratic deliberation requires restraint; it is not therapy for everybody's frustrations" (1998). Restraint is an essential part of deliberation so that discussion may continue.

Kingwell asserted that civil dialogue is a duty: "Civility is not only justifiable socially within a democracy, but also is in fact a crucial aspect of democracy, an internalization of the priority of right that is reflected in civil restrained conversation and the openness of tact—what I have labeled civil dialogue. To engage in this dialogue is the right and responsibility of every citizen" (1995, p. 243). This is not just a matter of expression of one's ideas but also entails thoughtful deliberation and tact. The classroom is a significant place in which to model democratic deliberation in open, thoughtful discussion structured within the curriculum.

Although the classroom does not necessarily operate as a democracy, there is an emphasis on reasoned expression and tolerance for opposing viewpoints for the common good, that being learning. For example, American University initiated an annual campuswide civility campaign, "Civitas" (from Latin for body-politic), including service-learning experience in the community, lectures, workshops, and individual projects, geared toward the interaction of faculty, staff, and students as a community. This is an example of an institution-supported project to encourage civic responsibility.

Because Civil Discourse Facilitates Understanding and Learning

Civil discourse encourages the respectful exchange of ideas. This type of interaction becomes a model for discussion in and outside the classroom and provides a measure of intellectual safety in which to deliberate. When open, thoughtful discussion is structured into the curriculum, students can observe the process of building understanding. For example, Head-Royce School in Oakland,

California, has instituted a Civic Purpose Committee to facilitate a year-long conversation among high school students about their attitudes toward civic responsibility. Peter Reinke, Director of Civic Purpose, specified the examination of public policy and development of leadership as outcomes of this undertaking. While deliberating about civic purpose, students have learned values as well as skills useful in future problem solving.

In addressing the Penn National Commission on Society, Culture and Community, Rodin referred to the "teachable moment...when the energy and passion combine with the honesty and the skill of intellectual inquiry to open the possibility of a transformational experience" or, as she would prefer to call it, "transformational discourse" (1997, p. 4). Every teacher has experienced a moment when classroom discussion has led to the "aha" moment of understanding the viewpoint of another, often connected to deep, long-lasting learning. Rodin also said, "We need to distinguish public conversation from public performance. Real conversation isn't simply displaying deeply held convictions—it presupposes a willingness to consider modifying them" (1998, p. 11). The classroom setting is an ideal place to model the process of modifying convictions by clarifying, listening, and deliberating toward understanding. Rodin wrote:

> The essence of civil discourse is the way it builds understanding. According to Kingwell, Tact is a basic requirement of civil discourse, the kind of talk in which politeness appears as an orientation toward understanding. By talking together in this restrained and receptive manner, two civil people can expect to understand one another and reach ever more general conclusions concerning their shared social space. Their dialogue serves to establish common ground between them, a basis for yet further understanding. (1995, p. 227)

Reaching understanding also establishes a foundation for future dialogue.

The other side of dialogue is listening. Business ethicist Robert Greenleaf said, "Listening might be defined as an attitude toward other people and what they are attempting to express. It includes constructive responses that help the other person express thoughts and feelings" (1996, p. 70). Listening improves face-to-face relations, but it is difficult to listen when one is defending one's own views.

Civil discourse in the classroom provides a model for civil discourse in the public sphere. In a review of literature on public discourse completed for the Penn National Commission, David Ryfe of the University of California, San Diego, identified the features of good public discourse. According to Ryfe (1998), traditionally, good public discourse has been considered to be simple rational argument, "impartial, disinterested, based in argument and evidence." However, "In the past twenty years, this view has come to be seen as overly sterile, exclusive, patriarchal and inadequate to describe the variety of motivations and forms that inspire public deliberation" (1998, p. 20). Ryfe suggested that we are moving "toward a conception of postmodern argument" that is characterized by formal democratic procedures, relationality and reason-giving, reflection, reciprocity, radical difference, and moderation. According to these principles, "individuals will advance arguments; they will link arguments to their personal experiences; they will be recognized as individuals with group affiliations rather than representatives of particular groups; and they will advance claims but also seek to establish commonality" (1998, p. 22).

In community colleges, which have a longstanding reputation for valuing the variety of experiences that highly diverse students bring to the classroom, collaborative learning is a well-used mode of instruction, a mode that creates an ideal setting for the promotion of civil discourse. As Ryfe pointed out, "Public discourse is as much about establishing and maintaining relationships as it is about winning arguments" (1998, p. 21). Thus, an important role of civility on a college campus is to clarify meanings and promulgate principles of good public discourse, mutual respect, and reflection. Civil discourse adds the dimension, either public or private, of receptivity and an orientation toward understanding other points of view.

In *Civility and Subversion*, Goldfarb (1998) defined civility as public discussion of pressing social problems and pointed out that the exchange of information is not necessarily discourse. Deliberation involves first reflecting about the information exchanged. Goldfarb also raised concern about the deleterious effect of cynicism on civil discourse. "The aim [of cynicism] is not to reason and illuminate, but to ridicule and entertain" (Goldfarb, 1998, p. 4). In order for civil discourse to predominate in the classroom, the instructor sets the tone for honesty, openness, good listening, thoughtful reflection, tact, sensitivity, and the avoidance of cynical remarks. Educational philosopher John Dewey spoke about "reflective morality," which involves conscious deliberation, reason, and thought. Civil discourse, when encouraged in the classroom, provides a platform for reasoned deliberation and opens the way to learning.

CHAPTER THREE

Strategies for Fostering Civility in the Classroom

Pressured by time to include sufficient content within an academic period, classroom faculty may be unwilling to discuss civility, other than to list rules for classroom behavior. In this chapter, I offer strategies for supporting civility.

Provide Orientation for New Students

Among public community college students, approximately 37% are first-generation students—that is, their parents have no postsecondary education experiences—and approximately 14% are foreign born (NCES, 2005). Attending college for the first time can be daunting for any new student, but for the many students who come from different countries or traditions, it is especially important to convey clear expectations for classroom behavior and to help them adjust. Students who are made to feel comfortable will be more willing to participate in classroom discussion and, hence, in learning.

A student's first impression of a campus and student support services can set the tone for the school year. Many colleges host campuswide orientation events offering information tables, welcome programs, refreshments, entertainment, and so forth. Formal orientation activities and orientation or guidance classes give colleges an opportunity to express a genuine welcome and openness, as well as to describe their expectations of the student. Orientation activities need to be coordinated and supported by the college. Community College of Baltimore County–Catonsville has developed a first-year course that focuses on academic skills as well as behaviors designed to help students be successful. Called "Achieving Academic Success," the course is not required but encouraged among first-year students.

In the classroom, it may be helpful for instructors to familiarize themselves with aspects of classroom behavior that relate to practices by those of a different culture. One good resource is *Multicultural Manners: New Rules of Etiquette for a Changing Society*, which includes a chapter on classroom behavior (Dresser, 1996). Helping students born outside the United States become adjusted to U.S. classrooms is less a matter of memorizing a variety of cultural rules than being open to understanding students from another culture. All students need to feel that their ideas will be respected. At the outset of a class, instructors should describe how class will be conducted and distribute any written guidelines, such as those for conducting civil discourse, that have been developed.

Teach Ethics and Civility as Course Subjects

Funded by the Carnegie and Rockefeller Funds, the Hastings Center, an independent, nonpartisan, and nonprofit bioethics research institute in New York, completed a systematic survey of the teaching of ethics and values in U.S. institutions of higher education. In the monograph, *Ethics in the Undergraduate Curriculum*, Rosen and Caplan (1980) discussed, among other things, the goals and content of an ethics course and whether students can learn ethical issues and values issues by the time they reach college. They differentiated courses that focus on metaethics, the discussion of theoretical questions and rational justifications, from those that focus on applied ethics in which discussion of issues and values takes place (and where discussion of responsibilities, rights, and civility would be most appropriate). They cited a variety of pedagogical methods, including video, film, panel discussions, lectures, case studies, and class projects as effective ways to treat the subject.

Rosen and Caplan suggested that instructors teaching ethics courses consider what the goal of the discussion is—to promote virtue, to change behavior, or to teach rational thinking—and whether the teaching can be done without indoctrinating students with the instructor's ideas. Instructors cannot effectively tell students to listen to discussions of ethics, but they can model openness in listening. Rosen and Caplan also recommended discussing the students' responsibilities by using examples that normally arise in class, such as attendance, missing assignments, or test performance. Instructors also can relate the discussion of individual responsibility to questions of civil state and civic virtue.

In *Ethics Teaching in Higher Education*, Callahan and Bok (1980) concluded their summary of the Hastings Center study by commending "experimental ethics" as a way of making morality a "lived experience." They recommended conducting a democratic classroom in which students can participate in fairness issues. For example, they described an ethics instructor who began his class by asking, "What are we doing here? What am I looking for from you? What are you looking for from me?" This discussion of course goals, according to Callahan and Bok, "leads to a contractual agreement" that entails a pragmatic democratic procedure and "sound educational practice from the standpoint of moral-development theory" (1980, p. 110).

Los Medanos College in California developed the course "Ethical Inquiry into Societal Issues," designed to "investigate societal issues using an interdisciplinary approach toward understanding the problems, possible options for solving the problems and the ethical choices involved in each issue and its resolution" (as per the course outline). A transferable and general education course that focuses on ethical aspects of controversial problems while engaging students in moral reasoning is required by Los Medanos. And an honors course, "Contemporary Issues: Reducing Public Health Disparities," is a variation of Philosophy 2 that covers ethical issues such as environmental protection, reproductive rights, genetic engineering, and affirmative action.

Embed Discussion of Ethics in Existing Curricula

Many colleges already have guidance classes such as "Orientation to College," providing instruction to first-year students on the resources of the college, and "College Success," providing instruction on developing traits that promote student success. Courses like these are ideal for including civility materials. The content of these courses is somewhat flexible, and they make ideal starting points for discussions of civility and expectations of classroom and campus interaction.

According to White, "Many areas of the curriculum—modern languages, geography, history, English—as well as, in many cases, the presence of diverse cultural groups in the classroom itself will provide opportunities to explore the expression of common values in different local mores" (1996, p. 87). For example, many social science lecture classes already include discussion of social behavior and individual responsibility; but ethical dimensions of such behavior could be emphasized in other introductory classes in disciplines such as history, philosophy, sociology, psychology, and social psychology—each of which addresses relationships between and among members of society—as well as in art classes, which promote the civilizing influence of art.

Science, especially biology, has received considerable attention as discoveries outstrip society's moral discussions about them. Keohane referred to "the dynamics of the classroom, conceiving it as a kind of public space where students should think about difficult issues of communication and listening, being sensitive to the points of view expressed by others" (1996, p. 4). Biology classes could address contemporary debate about scarce medical resources, cloning, and genetic engineering. Keohane also suggested that English courses could incorporate works of moral philosophy.

The teaching of values was put aside in public schools in the 1960s when strong controversy about what values to teach resulted in no values being formally taught. "Indeed, many faculty members express genuine alarm at the prospect of any consideration of ethical issues in regular courses," according to Callahan and Bok (1980, p. 196). With the horror of recent violence and shootings in schools, the topic of character education has reappeared in the national conversation (Jacobs, 1999). Character education, as it is recently called, is a set of values determined by teachers and parents and taught to students as community standards.

Santa Clara University's Markkula Center for Applied Ethics (www.scu.edu/ethics) teaches "educators how to incorporate values in their teaching" (Jacobs, 1999, p. 7). Several local high schools have participated in the program, which includes an instructor who uses the Socratic method to impart ethics as part of literature in his English courses. McEwen recommended that instructors "teach rules of civil behavior. In college classrooms, develop rules and disseminate them to class members as part of an assignment" (1997, p. 2). She also spoke of having students discuss how breaches of civility are handled in different cultures within the United States and in other countries, using library or Internet research and in-person interviews.

Incorporate Civility Into Classroom and Campus Activities

In *Among Friends*, Dalton and Watson (1997) described classrooms where caring and learning prevail as a way to promote civility. Although the book is designed for K–12 education, several useful principles could be adapted for learning by adults. They cited research showing that "high school students had higher interest in schooling, gains in mathematics achievement, better attendance, and lower drop-out rates when their schools functioned as communities with shared values, common activities, and personalized caring relationships among members" (1997, p. 164). For example, while addressing content, they suggested using community-building exercises, such as having students interview one another, work in groups as collaborative learning mechanisms, and apply classroom rules developed by the students that focus on treatment by other members of the class.

The Professional & Organizational Development Network in Higher Education Web site published a series of eight scholarly essays on teaching excellence. In one essay, "Academic Civility Begins in the Classroom," there is an excellent section called "Promoting Civility in the Classroom" (Baldwin, 2007), which not only outlines core principles for classroom civility but also suggests a variety of instructional modes and activities that can be used effectively to teach or model civility. These activities include staging debates, role playing and role reversal, case studies, and critiquing negative models. (The essay can be viewed online; see the reference list for the URL). The Calibrated Review Project at University of California, Los Angeles is a Web-based program that enables students to review and discuss the work of their peers, and they are instructed in the use of honesty and tact while doing so. Although the project stems from a science-based model, it is discipline- and level-independent.

In *Generation X Goes to College*, Sacks (1996) painted a rather negative picture of college students but laid the blame primarily on postmodern society, which he described as anti-rationalist and having a hyperconsumer mentality. He recommended that college instructors adapt to the technology orientation of so-called Gen Xers by becoming less lecturers than facilitators for applying knowledge. Sacks used examples such as teacher-as-consultant in a compact disc for a lab class and posting for discussion one's term paper on a Web site. Another way of embedding civility in courses using technology is to teach students to use the principles of civil discourse in their chat room conversations in distance education courses.

Callahan and Bok recommended democratizing the wider program or school by giving students the opportunity "to have input into decisions about course requirements, program policies, and the like" (1980, p. 18), much as San Jose/Evergreen Community College District colleges do by inviting students to be members of college committees. Callahan and Bok also recommended providing "opportunities for students to step into roles of social responsibility for real-world problems in the larger community" (1980, p. 118), as numerous community colleges do through experiential service-learning programs. Additional support for classroom and co-curricular activities as providing development of community mindedness comes from Long:

> Classroom activities provide an opportunity for community just as important, although different in form, as what happens outside the classroom walls. It is frequently assumed that a class is merely a group of entirely private individuals having obligations only to their teacher....But if a classroom is viewed as a learning community, students will see doing assignments on time as crucial to the dynamics of learning. (1992, p. 50)

Offer Special Civility-Related Training

The Baltimore Sun (Dechter, 2007) reported on American University's "campus-wide civility campaign branded *Civitas*." This annual week-long event, which includes lectures and workshops for the university community, has generated much interest, and Civitas co-chair Bernard Schulz has been asked "to make presentations on their effort to higher education institutions around the country, from Wyoming's higher education commission to Georgetown University and Loyola College in Baltimore."

Two other examples of civility-specific training are described in the appendix. One is a professional development workshop called "Promoting Civility on Campus," offered by the online educational organization StudentAffairs.com. The other is a series of empowerment workshops, held by Hudson Valley Community College in New York to help students understand and meet the institution's expectations (see appendix, pages 42–44).

> "Teachers are committed to developing and actively protecting a class environment in which respect must be shown to everyone in order to facilitate and encourage expression, testing, understanding, and creation of a variety of ideas and opinions. Any successful learning experience requires mutual respect on behalf of the students and the instructor. The instructor, as well as fellow students, should not be subjected to any student's behavior that is in any way disruptive or rude. A student should not feel intimidated or demeaned by his/her instructor and students must remember that the instructor has primary responsibility for control over classroom behavior and maintenance of academic integrity.—Teaching and Learning Center, University of Nebraska-Lincoln"

Model Civility as an Instructor

Nel Noddings, the Lee L. Jacks Professor of Education, Emerita, at Stanford University, is closely associated with the ethics of care in education, which involves "stepping out of one's own personal frame of reference into another's" (2005b, p. 24). She sees behavior in the classroom not defined and conditioned by rules but situated in ethics and underlying respect. During a lecture on caring among teachers, Noddings (1998) established a relationship between caring, which she sees as a virtue, and teacher competence (in addition to subject matter competence). According to Noddings, "A caring teacher must possess a set of qualities that we rightly call virtues or excellences" (1998).

Noddings believes that teacher–student interaction must be infused with caring, reciprocity, and respect. She said, "the teacher bears a special responsibility for the enhancement of the ethical ideal. She is often in contact with the ethical ideal as it is being initially constructed, and, even with the adult student, she has unique power contributing to its enhancement or destruction" (1984, p. 178). This role is a self-conscious one, and teachers must examine their own stance toward providing moral guidance. The formation of values occurs in the classroom concomitantly with the imparting of subject matter. This implies the necessity of awareness on the part of a teacher to model the values and virtues that he or she considers important. According to Noddings, "What is learned from caring teachers willing to share their knowledge and their pleasure in learning is often incidental and very powerful precisely because it is given freely" (2005a). Civility and caring are part of this modeling.

Forni is also concerned about the role instructors play in imparting civility. Commenting that teachers can have a negative effect on students, Forni (2002) has said, "As we talk about incivility among the student body, we should also talk about incivility among the teaching body." Forni believes that teachers can be overbearing and "adopt behavior that can mortify students." He explained that, "They (faculty) can exhibit a purported intellectual superiority, belittle students, and use sarcasm in a way that can be hurtful." As a faculty member himself, Forni exhorts fellow faculty members to look to themselves as models for civility in the classroom. This notion of personal responsibility should also permeate the administration and top levels of college leadership, as all citizens and staff members are capable both of displaying incivility and modeling civility.

University of Washington education professor Walter Parker has written about teaching children life skills. In "The Art of Deliberation" (1997), he gave tips on nurturing civility for different age groups of students within the K–12 system. Reviewing classroom materials on nurturing civility, three key actions emerged:

1. Increase the variety and frequency of interaction among students who are different from one another.
2. Orchestrate these contacts to foster deliberation about two common kinds of problems: those that arise from the friction of interaction itself and those grounded in the academic controversies at the core of each discipline.
3. Clarify the distinction between deliberation and blather. In other

words, expect, teach, and model competent deliberation that is rooted
in knowledge. (Parker, 1997, p. 19)

Deliberation, said Parker, should not be confused with debate, which is
defending pre-formed opinions, or with "alternating monologues, where there is
sequential talking but no real listening let alone empathy" (1997, p. 20). So,
deliberation teaches students to think and exchange ideas—but to do so with
civility. Parker also emphasized the importance of what he called "the deliberative
arts," which include

> Many facets of joint problem solving — listening as well as talking,
> grasping others' points of view, and using the common space to
> forge positions with others rather than using it only as a platform
> for expressing opinions. Acquired long before, this blend of
> skills, dispositions, and knowledge is what enables a diverse
> group of people—young or old—to peacefully discuss divisive
> issues in order to forge an intelligent and just decision that is
> binding on all. Such education in schools helps children develop
> the public virtues. (1997, p. 22)

Parker suggested that teacher education incorporate the use of the deliberative
arts as a step in modeling behavior for students.

One article in a series on civility that appears in the "Thriving in
Academe" section of the National Education Association Web site stresses the
importance of modeling decorous behavior right from the start (see appendix,
page 45). Richardson (1999) also assembled a variety of experts in instruction to
discuss civil classroom behavior in *Promoting Civility: A Teaching Challenge*. In
the book, Tiberius and Flak explicate "behavioral aspects of the teacher-learner
alliance," in which they discuss the building of relationships through steps of
negotiation. A thorough examination of the classroom climate and values is
contributed by Anderson, who said "the college classroom must appear safe and
coercion-free in order to produce optimal participation and minimal disruption"
(p. 71). Richardson suggested that in order to promote civility, instructors must
be aware of their own values.

In *Civic Virtues and Public Schooling*, White (1996), referring to K–12
education, stressed the importance of teachers knowing their own values in
relation to their school community and structuring ways to communicate them:

Teachers need time to reflect on [community] issues and the delicate matter of applying them to the educational situations in which they find themselves. Just as important, they need time to discuss with colleagues how the school community should be structured as an institution in which students can become hopeful, confident, courageous, honest, self-respecting citizens with appropriate self-esteem. (1996, p. 89)

"Since every student is entitled to full participation in class without interruption, all students are expected to be in class and prepared to begin on time. All pagers, wireless phones, electronic games, radios, tape or CD players or other devices that generate sound must be turned off when you enter the classroom. Disruption of class, whether by latecomers, noisy devices or inconsiderate behavior will not be tolerated. Repeated violations will be penalized and may result in expulsion from the class.— civility clause required on all syllabi at Eastfield College in Dallas"

Establish Guidelines for Classroom Conduct and Civil Discourse

A 1998 study in Baltimore-area schools conducted by Jim McPartland of Johns Hopkins University speculated that students want the rules of civility. Part of the study involved the measurement of cursing in public areas of the school. McPartland noted that students were more likely to curse at one another than at teachers. "They clearly knew the difference," he said. He believes that schools can cut down on rudeness and create a sense of civility by establishing a personalized, caring environment and reducing anonymity. At one school in the study, a "whole school" concept was developed that included tutorial and personal assistance in the context of school-work-careers, and efforts were made to know students by their first names.

Mary Deane Sorcinelli (2003–2004) at the University of Massachusetts Amherst has written suggestions for faculty dealing with incivility, urging them to establish clear rules, to discuss them on the first day of class, and to discuss classroom etiquette. Suggestions included connecting with students by learning their names, having them fill out questionnaires, and making frequent eye contact. She further recommended that teachers come to class early, "work the aisles," and give students an opportunity to talk one-on-one (The complete article,

"Encouraging Civil Behavior in Large Classes," can be viewed online; see the reference list for the URL).

However, to merely enumerate rules without discussion of individual responsibility as it relates to respect for others does not encourage students to integrate their understanding of the underlying civility and to transfer this concept to other venues. In a project to introduce civility in the classroom (Rookstool, 2003), students' ratings of classroom behavior demonstrated an increased awareness of civility among students in their classrooms following a discussion of its tenets. (The report on this project, *Civility: Can It Be Taught In The Classroom?*, is available from the author; see the references for contact information.) The classroom behaviors rated included the following, which can also serve as a model for civil discourse guidelines:

- listeners facing speaker
- speaker summarizing ideas of previous speaker
- speakers using neutral or positive tone of voice
- listeners and speakers exhibiting neutral facial expression
- speakers' comments focusing on issues not persons
- speakers' points are supported by reasons
- speakers taking turns to avoid interruptions
- speakers using respectful words or verbal strategies (i.e., "Please clarify," "I'm unclear about," "I disagree because," "In other words, you are saying") speakers indicating understanding of another's ideas even if they disagree

Although apparently developed as a tool for guiding discussion in public forums, the guidelines for civil discourse developed by the town of Lexington, Massachusetts, provide a good model for conducting civil discourse in the classroom setting (see appendix, page 46). Forni's 25 rules of considerate conduct (see Forni, 2002) exemplify principles of civility appropriate to both the classroom and society. (To view the rules, which are listed in the table of contents of Forni's book, see the listing on Amazon.com.) Currently, Forni is working on a new book on rudeness, with a chapter on academia, but he is cognizant of the importance of civility to students' futures, as well. In an interview in *The Baltimore Sun* Forni said, "Improving 'relational skills' on campus is important not just to foster a better learning environment, but to prepare students for the workforce" (Dechter, 2007).

"De Anza College shall take all steps necessary to provide a positive educational and employment environment, which encourages equal educational opportunities. The college will actively seek to educate staff and students on the deleterious effects of expressions of hatred or contempt based on race, color, national or ethnic origin, age, gender, religion, sexual orientation, marital status, or physical or psychological disability; and will promote equality and mutual respect and understanding among all groups and individuals."—De Anza College Catalog, 2006

Adopt Formal Statements on Civility and Ethics

A statement describing civility and an expectation of mutual respect should be incorporated in a variety of campus publications, including the college catalog, schedule, and individual course syllabi. Mission statements, as well as appropriate policies and procedures of colleges, should include campus-developed statements of civility and civil discourse. Civility statements can come in many forms and should be addressed to many areas. Examples from the following three colleges are included in the appendix. Each contextualizes a list of rules within the concept of civility and responsibility to others.

Jamestown Community College in New York outlines student rights in its civility statement, but then it focuses on desirable and undesirable classroom behavior. The civility statement of Bloomfield College, an independent four-year college in New Jersey, also encompasses human dignity and explicitly cites protected minorities and forbidden behaviors. The Campus Civility Statement of Coe College, an independent four-year institution in Cedar Rapids, Iowa, was written by students and is oriented to community-building.

The University of California, Davis has a civility statement that it calls "Principles of Community," a title that illustrates the interrelatedness of citizenship and civility (see appendix, pages 47–51). Some colleges have adopted lists of core values rather than civility statements per se, which function as operational tenets of citizenship and civil discourse. For example, in 1987, the Florida State University System adopted a list of values, introducing them with the statement, "These values and principles are specific enough to be meaningful and broad enough to be acceptable in a pluralistic culture (Eberly, 1994). Fifteen values were stated:

1. Personal integrity that is rooted in respect for truth and love of learning.
2. A sense of duty to self, family, and to the larger community.

3. Self-esteem rooted in the quest for the achievement of one's potential.

4. Respect for the rights of all persons regardless of their race, religion, nationality, sex, and age, physical condition, or mental state.

5. The courage to express one's convictions, and the recognition of the rights of others to hold and express differing views.

6. The capacity to make discriminating judgments among competing opinions.

7. A sense of, and commitment to, justice, rectitude, and fair play.

8. Understanding, sympathy, concern, and compassion for others.

9. A sense of discipline and pride in one's work; respect for achievements of others.

10. Respect for one's property and the property of others, including public property.

11. An understanding of, and appreciation for, other cultures and traditions.

12. A willingness to perform the obligations of citizenship, including the obligation to cast an informed ballot, to complete jury service, to participate in government, and to respect the rule of law.

13. Civility, including congenial relations between men and women.

14. A commitment to academic freedom as a safeguard essential to the purposes of the college and to the welfare of those who work for it.

15. The courage to oppose the use of substances which impair one's judgment or one's health. (Eberly, 1994)

"It might be very tempting to not do anything about incivility in your classroom and simply hope that the incident does not reoccur. However, you could be interfering with other student's learning in the class if you allow the behavior to continue."—Holladay (2006)

Develop Strategies and Guidelines for Addressing Incivility

In an article for *The Chronicle of Higher Education*, Schneider (1998) surveyed a variety of educational institutions struggling with issues of civility. She noted a concern by many educators with a rise in uncivil behavior among students followed by specific actions. For example, Montana State University created a task force to examine disruptive behavior; the Virginia Polytechnic Institute Faculty Senate initiated a "Climate Committee" to study undergraduate "insolence"; Indiana University formed a "Committee for a Respectful Learning

Environment"; and Johns Hopkins University introduced a course entitled "Civility, Manners, and Politeness."

I have found two good resources on managing incivility. One is an article posted on the University of Texas at Austin Web site (see Holladay, 2006) that defines classroom incivility, analyzes its causes, and offers educators concrete suggestions for dealing with it. Another is an article that outlines ways of dealing with specific kinds of troublesome classroom behavior, including the following:

- talking and inattention
- unpreparedness, missed deadlines and tests, and fraudulent excuse making
- lateness and inattendance
- challenges to authority
- overt hostility from a student (Reed, 2007; see reference list for a URL to the complete article)

For a college to foster an atmosphere of civility, there must first be a conscious decision to do so. As simple as that sounds, such a decision supercedes piecemeal efforts by instructors to incorporate rules of behavior into their course descriptions or by student services to offer selected orientation classes. This must be a multifaceted, coordinated process, supported by all segments of the institution. The University of California, Davis, for example, forged a statement of the overarching importance of community, which at the same time recognizes the freedom of each teacher to determine the course of civility. The very process of creating this statement of principles involved open, thoughtful discussion and deliberation, in itself an act of civility. An excerpt is printed here, with key words in boldface (see appendix, page 51, for the complete statement):

We affirm the right of **freedom of expression** within our community and affirm our commitment to the highest standards of **civility** and decency towards all. We recognize the right of every individual to think and speak as dictated by personal belief, to **express** any idea, and to disagree with or counter another's point of view, limited only by university regulations governing time, place and manner. We promote open expression of our individuality and our **diversity** within the bounds of **courtesy**, **sensitivity** and **respect**.

The Penn National Commission on Society, Culture and Community developed a list of implications for improving public discourse as a part of its concluding report. The Commission specified the "need for a more active and self-conscious effort—a national movement—to foster a public culture that supports the building of strong, inclusive communities through substantive, honest, productive public conversation" (2000). Although every institution must decide for itself the transformation to civility, the strategies described in this chapter may assist in this unfolding.

CHAPTER FOUR

Conclusion and Recommendations

The Ideal Classroom

A classroom in which civility is encouraged gives students opportunities for constructing knowledge (content) as well as developing skills essential for social interaction (process) as citizens in the community. Ideally, a teacher fostering such a learning environment would draw upon best practices from a variety of settings. Ideas might come from professional development training, colleagues, written material, videotapes, podcasts, a Web site, or something not yet invented.

In an ideal classroom setting, there would be a variety of views expressed by a diversity of participants. The instructor would, minimally, set forth explicit expectations of mutual respect and civil discourse, and, ideally, foster discussions about the importance of civility, respect, and discourse in a classroom setting. The instructor would model respect for ideas, students, and colleagues; distinguish personal opinion from fact; provide opportunities for students to use civil discourse; and give feedback on classroom discussions.

Learning activities that support students' getting to know one another, including students from different cultural backgrounds, would be used throughout the semester. If collaborative learning techniques were employed, there would be some discussion of how students should act within a small group. Peer tutoring could be organized in a one-to-one or small group setting, so that students further learn to help one another. The student should have ample chance for problem solving, reflection, peer review, and evaluation of content and process.

Outside the classroom, there should be opportunities for experience-based learning, as well as for participation in campus- and community-based activities, such as service-learning and learning communities. In co-curricular activities, students would be encouraged to participate in leadership development and governance aspects of the college. At the college, there would be a variety of events and speakers in an environment that challenges thinking and opinions. The college would continue to support community mentorship programs as well as develop faculty mentorship and professional development. The college would sponsor campus educational and social events through which the entire campus community could participate and learn. There would be frequent and public recognition of contributions to campus and community.

In an ideal classroom setting, an instructor would have adopted a well-considered ethical stance and would employ it through interaction with students. Encouraging civility in the classroom is not about providing some contrived community of shared values that exist for a moment in time (16-week semester); it is about setting a tone for the college community of mutual respect and civil discourse. This is as true for math as it is philosophy, for art as it is for guidance.

Recommendations

Classroom Related

1. Develop for inclusion in course syllabi a statement delineating expectations of civility, mutual respect, and civil conduct in the classroom.
2. Set aside at least one class at the beginning of an academic period for discussing expectations for open dialogue, mutual respect, and civility.
3. Use opportunities to both model and employ the use of mutual respect, open dialogue, and civil discourse in classroom discussion.
4. Consider, where appropriate, use of activities that allow students to know one another; consider use of collaborative learning and group projects.
5. Include civility-related topics in college orientation classes and other courses, where appropriate.
6. Create a compendium of best classroom practices suggested by staff, which encourage civility and civil discourse.
7. Develop an applied ethics or social issues course, perhaps using a multidisciplinary approach. Consider including civility-related topics in existing courses such as sociology, philosophy, psychology, and guidance classes.
8. Create a Web-based instructional service site, which provides advice on a variety of classroom instructional techniques, for example, the development of course outlines, and pedagogical strategies such as collaborative learning and group discussion models emphasizing civil discourse.

Campus Related

1. Review campus publications for appropriate insertion of language that encourages civility. Such language could appear in the college mission statement, Web site, catalog, schedule of classes, and selected brochures.

2. Consider the use of staff development or college funds to sponsor a workshop for staff, and possibly for others in the education community, on civility and civil discourse in the classroom.

3. Consider the use of staff development or college funds to sponsor a forum or series of lectures that encourage and model principles of civil discourse, for discussion of issues in ethics and applied ethics.

4. Develop an instructor-mentoring program, noting opportunities for encouraging new teachers to apply principles of civil discourse in the classroom.

5. Periodically administer a collegewide campus climate survey to evaluate campus attitudes on an ongoing basis.

6. Coordinate activities surrounding the first week of classes to ensure a friendly, caring, and welcoming environment and to set a tone for civility on campus.

7. Emphasize the principle of community or public service for staff and students. Introduce or expand a service-learning project. Encourage students to relate community service to common core values and their own individual values.

8. Post signs in public areas of the college, such as the cafeteria, library, theater, community room, college conference room, gymnasiums, stadium, and parking lots extolling respect and civility.

9. Offer staff training, especially to staff members who have initial or frequent contact with students, to revitalize and maintain civil practices on campus.

10. Encourage faculty to become advisors to student clubs, and to associations that develop civic participation.

11. Recognize contributions of all types by individuals to the campus and community.

Related to Public Space

1. In conjunction with new campus construction, increase public meeting spaces and establish visually well-defined entrances to the campus. Include ways for staff and students to participate in discussion of new spaces, especially at the program development stage.

2. Improve public spaces on campus with art, colorful surroundings, cultural performances, comfortable seating, and meaningful signage. Encourage grounds staff to continue and maintain improvements in landscaping.

3. Develop a graffiti removal task force that can respond quickly to problems.

Appendix: Examples and Models

Online Civility Course—StudentAffairs.com

Civility Workshop—Hudson Valley Community College

Classroom Best Practices—National Education Association

Guidelines for Civil Discourse—Lexington, MA

Civility Guidelines—Jamestown Community College

Civility Statement—Bloomfield College

Civility Statement—Coe College

Civility Statement—University of California, Davis

Online Civility Course—StudentAffairs.com

Promoting Civility on Campus

Course Outline

The course is divided into three modules, concluding with a list of "best practices" for promoting civility on campus. The first module focuses on how civility might be defined and whether colleges should have any role in promoting it. The second module explores the possible regulation of offensive or uncivil expression, including "hate speech" and profanity. The third module will consider broader, environmental approaches to promoting civility inside and outside the classroom.

Learning Outcomes

Active participants in the course will

- Review and evaluate competing definitions of civility
- Explore the value and purpose of civility in campus life
- Learn distinctions between unlawful harassment and expression protected by the First Amendment
- Examine ways civility can be promoted inside and outside the classroom
- Consider ways students can become active participants in defining and promoting civility
- Receive a list of "best practices" for promoting civility on campus

Participant Expectations

Participants will be expected to devote approximately fifteen hours to the course (five hours for each of the three week modules). Assignments will include selected readings and discussions. Active participation in online discussions will enhance learning outcomes. At the close of the course, each participant will be asked to submit a short list of at least three "best practices" for promoting civility on campus, drawn from course (or personal) readings, or their own professional experience.

Note. From StudentAffairs.com. (2007). *Promoting civility on campus* [Course outline]. Retrieved February 9, 2007, from www.studentaffairs.com/onlinecourses/winter2006course8.html

Civility Workshop— Hudson Valley Community College

Civility, Conduct, and Respect at Hudson Valley Community College: What's Expected of Me?

Hudson Valley Community College values freedom of speech and expression in the academic arena. As a diverse community of learners, we must create an academic environment that encourages individual freedoms, and at the same time guarantees minimal distractions when participating in the learning process. A code of classroom etiquette must be employed in order to ensure civility, tolerance and mutual respect within all academic settings.

Collaboration among faculty, staff and students is imperative for a successful and welcoming educational environment. Civility is dedicated to establishing partnerships that will allow faculty, staff and students to share their experiences and thoughts about teaching and learning.

Civility is linked to the Latin word *civitas*, which means "city" and "community." Thus, civility implies a larger social concern. When we are civil we are members in good standing of a community. We are good neighbors and good citizens. Whether we look at the core of manners or civility we discern not only pleasant form but ethical substance as well.

Culture Shock

"Culture Shock" is a one-hour, interactive workshop designed to help students adjust to the academic expectations and social pressures of college life. This workshop helps participants to

- Acclimate successfully to Hudson Valley Community College.
- Address expectations of the higher education experience.
- Increase awareness of the skills and behaviors necessary to thrive in a college setting.
- Learn about the various student services available.
- Ask questions and voice concerns about the transition to Hudson Valley Community College.

Men's Workshop

The "Men's Workshop" is a one-hour interactive, informal meeting designed to help male students meet their mental, physical, emotional and spiritual needs as they strive for academic excellence. This workshop helps participants to

- Achieve a sense of balance in their lives.
- Address how notions of masculinity affect their self-perception.
- Increase awareness of how their actions affect their surrounding environment.

Respect: Part I

"Respect: Part I" is a one-hour participatory workshop designed to increase sensitivity and awareness of how our behavior affects those around us. This workshop helps participants to

- Think about how they define respect.
- Think about how definitions of respect may vary between individuals, generations and cultures.
- Recognize and appreciate their similarities and differences.

Respect: Part II

"Respect: Part II" is a one-hour participatory workshop designed to increase sensitivity and awareness of how our behavior affects those around us. This workshop is a continuation of "Respect: Part I." This workshop helps participants to

- Think about how they define respect.
- Think about how definitions of respect may vary between individuals, generations and cultures.
- Recognize and appreciate their similarities and differences.
- Identify ways they can help improve a sense of community on campus.

Note. From Hudson Valley Community College. (2007). *Civility, conduct, and respect at Hudson Valley Community College: What's expected of me?* [Workshop description]. https://www.hvcc.edu/civility/index.html

Classroom Best Practices—
National Education Association

How to Create Classroom Decorum by Modeling It

The best time to set expectations is at the start of a course as you and the students are getting to know each other. Consider the following strategies:

- Make behavioral expectations clear in your syllabus. Use positive, constructive language, not threats of reprisal.
- Talk about yourself. Let your students hear what you value.
- Learn about your students. Ask about their hopes and concerns.
- Earn trust by being trustworthy. Live up to your own expectations and be consistent in applying them to students.
- Prepare students for active learning by encouraging them to see learning as a process, not a product.
- Use collaborative projects and group dialogue as an opportunity for students to set and meet expectations for themselves.
- Model adult behavior. Remember that "apprentice" adults take many of their tacit cues from respected mentors.
- Be alert for symptoms of mismatched expectations. Even minor incivility should not be ignored, but treated as a sign that realignment of expectations is needed.
- Be prepared to adjust your own behavior, if necessary, and to let students learn from your example.
- Take time to discuss your expectations with other teachers. The faculty development center on your campus may sponsor seminars or informal opportunities to learn how other teachers approach civility issues in their classrooms.

Note. National Education Association and Professional & Occupational Development Network. (2007). Best practices: How to create classroom decorum by modeling it. In *Thriving in Academe* [Online forum]. Retrieved February 9, 2007, from www2.nea.org/he/advo00/advo0003/bestprac.html

Guidelines for Civil Discourse— Lexington, MA

The Town of Lexington (Massachusetts) respects and recognizes each citizen's right to free speech. In order to guarantee all people's right to free speech and to ensure productive civil discourse, we request that all citizens respect the following guidelines.

Show respect for others.
- Discuss policies and ideas, not people.
- Only one person should be speaking at any given time.
- Use helpful, not hurtful, language.

Speak as you would like to be spoken to.
- Use courtesy titles (Mr., Ms., Sir, etc.)
- Restate ideas when asked.
- Use a civil tone of voice.

Agree to listen.
- Respectfully hear and listen to differing points of view.
- When unsure, clarify what you heard.
- Realize that what you say and what people understand you to have said may be different.
- Recognize that people can agree to disagree.

Speak for yourself, not others.
- Speak from your own experience.
- Use "I" statements ("I think that the ideas presented …").

Follow agreed upon guidelines regarding who speaks when and for how long.

Note. From Town of Lexington. (2007). *Guidelines for civil discourse.* Retrieved February 9, 2007, from http://ci.lexington.ma.us/NoPlace4Hate/CivilDiscourse.htm

Civility Guidelines—
Jamestown Community College

Classroom Civility Guide for Students

Civility Statement

Jamestown Community College is committed to the highest standards of academic and ethical integrity, acknowledging that respect for self and others is the foundation of educational excellence. As such, we will cultivate an environment of mutual respect and responsibility. Whether we are students, faculty, or staff, we have a right to be in a safe environment, free of disturbance and civil in all aspects of human relations.

Expectations of Students in the Classroom

Your academic attitude is a major factor in your success at Jamestown Community College. You share responsibility, along with your professor and other students, for creating a productive learning environment. This responsibility includes behaving courteously and respectfully toward your professors and your classmates and becoming self-disciplined in your learning. To create a productive college experience for you and all students, you should:

- Attend class and pay attention. Do not ask the instructor to go over material you missed by skipping class or not concentrating. If you have difficulty understanding the presented material, ask the instructor to assist you.
- Not come to class late or leave early. If you must enter late, do so quietly and do not disrupt the class by walking between the class and the instructor. Do not leave class early unless it is an absolute necessity. If you know in advance you will need to leave class early, sit near an exit and inform the instructor prior to class.
- Not talk with other classmates while the instructor or another student is speaking. If you have a question or comment, please raise your hand, rather than start a conversation with your neighbor. Others in the class may have the same question.
- Show respect and concern for others by not monopolizing class discussion. Allow others time to give their input and ask questions. Do not stray from the topic of class discussion.

- Turn off all electronic devices, including but not limited to cell phones, pagers, beeping watches. If, due to work or family obligations, you need to remain in contact, inform your instructor ahead of time and set these devices to be as unobtrusive as possible.
- Avoid audible and visible signs of restlessness. These are both rude and disruptive to the rest of the class.
- Focus on class material during class time. Sleeping, talking to others, doing work for another class, reading the newspaper, checking e-mail, exploring the Internet, etc., are unacceptable and can be disruptive.
- Not pack bookbags or backpacks to leave until the instructor has dismissed the class.
- Clear any visitors you would like to bring to class with your instructor ahead of time.

Your Rights as a Student

As a student, you have the right to a learning environment free from distractions. If others in your classroom are engaging in behavior that interferes with your learning, bring the situation to the attention of your instructor. He or she is responsible for managing the classroom environment and determining the action that should be taken.

Consequences of Inappropriate Classroom Behavior

The instructor has the right and the responsibility to take appropriate action when he or she observes an instance of inappropriate classroom behavior. The form of intervention taken by the instructor will depend on the nature of the misconduct observed. The Constitution of the Student Body outlines the process to be followed and sanctions that may be placed on students who engage in various forms of misconduct.

A Final Note

The college is committed to creating and maintaining an effective community of learners in which all can grow and develop. We look forward to interacting with you in a civil and respectful classroom environment that encourages dialogue, supports the acquisition of knowledge, and assists all students in meeting their academic and personal goals.

Note. From Jamestown Community College. (2007). *Classroom civility guide for students.* Retrieved February 9, 2007, from www.sunyjcc.edu/college-wide/studentinfo/ civilityguidestudents.htm

Civility Statement—Bloomfield College

Division of Student Affairs—Statement on Civility and Human Dignity

The mission of Bloomfield College is "to prepare students to attain academic, personal and professional excellence in a multiracial and global society." It is fundamental to our mission to create an unbiased community and to oppose vigorously any form of racism, religious intolerance, sexism, ageism, homophobia, heterosexism, and discrimination against those with disabling conditions. As the College recognizes the presence of gays, lesbians and bisexuals as members of our community, we therefore affirm the legitimacy and right of gays, lesbians, and bisexuals to create and enrich their cultural experience on our campus.

Consistent with this belief, discrimination and/or harassment based upon sexual orientation are prohibited. These include, but are not limited to, the following acts, even if communicative in nature. Each of the following are prohibited and could result in charges that could lead to the full range of sanctions, including suspension or expulsion from the College, under the College Code of Student Conduct.

1. Use of force against the person or property of any member of the College Community, or against the person or property of anyone on College premises, or the threat of such physical abuse.
2. Theft of, or intentional damage to, College property or property in the possession of, or owned by, any member of the College.
3. Harassment, which is statutorily defined by New Jersey law to mean, and here means, purposefully making or causing to be made a communication or communications anonymously or at extremely inconvenient hours, or in offensively coarse language, or in any other manner likely to cause annoyance or alarm, or subjecting or threatening to subject another to striking, kicking, shoving or other offensive touching, or engaging in any other course of conduct of repeatedly committed acts with purpose to alarm or seriously annoy any other person.
4. Defamation, which is judicially defined to mean, and here means, the unprivileged oral or written publication of a false statement of fact that exposes the person about whom it is made to hatred, contempt or ridicule, or subjects the person to loss of the goodwill and

confidence of others, or so harms that person's reputation as to deter others from associating with her or him.

While any of the four categories of acts listed could lead to the full range of sanctions as listed in the Code of Conduct, clearly minor instances of such prohibited behavior could be resolved at the Dean level. The initial judgments of the nature of such an act or acts are to be made by the appropriate Dean. Students believing themselves to be victims of behaviors as suggested above, should contact the Dean of Students. Faculty, believing themselves to be victims of these behaviors, should contact the Dean of Academic Affairs. All other persons should contact the Affirmative Action Officer.

Note. From Bloomfield College. (2007). *Statement on civility and human dignity.* Retrieved February 9, 2007 from www.bloomfield.edu/studentaffairs/civility2.asp

Civility Statement—Coe College

We, the members of the Coe College community, expect our campus climate to be safe, mutually supportive, academically encouraging, egalitarian, and tolerant of all its members:

- We expect the academic experience to extend beyond the classroom into our living environment.
- We expect a campus free of incidents that create a hostile living environment.
- We expect a healthy and responsible attitude to accompany all social gatherings.
- We expect that intoxication will not be an excuse for incidents that occur while under the influence.
- We expect that diversity of opinion should be cultivated and encouraged as well as respected within our community.
- We expect that everyone will have the right to be respected for his or her individuality.
- We expect all campus community members to respect the rights of other persons regardless of their actual or perceived age, color, creed, disability, gender identity, national origin, race, religion, sex, or sexual orientation.

A community is made up of individuals who model these standards and hold each other accountable. In order for the community to encompass the goals outlined above, each individual must be responsible and accountable for her or his own actions and words.

Note. From Coe College. (2007). Campus civility statement. Retrieved February 9, 2007, from www.coe.edu/reslife/handbook/index.htm

Civility Statement—
University of California, Davis

The Principles of Community

The University of California at Davis is first and foremost an institution of learning and teaching, committed to serving the needs of society. Our campus community reflects and is a part of a society comprising all races, creeds, and social circumstances. The successful conduct of the University's affairs requires that every member of the University community acknowledge and practice the following basic principles:

We affirm the dignity inherent in all of us, and we strive to maintain a climate of justice marked by respect for each other. We acknowledge that our society carries within it historical and deep-rooted misunderstandings and biases, and therefore we will endeavor to foster mutual understanding among the many parts of our whole.

We affirm the right of freedom of expression within our community and also affirm our commitment to the highest standards of civility and decency towards all. We recognize the right of every individual to think and speak as dictated by personal belief, to express any idea, and to disagree with or counter another's point of view, limited only by University regulations governing time, place, and manner. We promote open expression of our individuality and our diversity within the bounds of courtesy, sensitivity, and respect.

We confront and reject all manifestations of discrimination, including those based on race, ethnicity, gender, age, disability, sexual orientation, religious or political beliefs, status within or outside the University, or any of the other differences among people which have been excuses for misunderstanding, dissension, or hatred. We recognize and cherish the richness contributed to our lives by our diversity. We take pride in our various achievements, and we celebrate our differences.

We recognize that each of us has an obligation to the community of which we have chosen to be a part. We will strive to build a true community of spirit and purpose based on mutual respect and caring.

Note. From University of California, Davis. (2007). *The principles of community*. Retrieved February 9, 2007, from http://principles.ucdavis.edu

References

Achacoso, M. V. (2002). *What do you mean my grade is not an A?: An investigation of academic entitlement, causal attributions, and self-regulation in college students.* Unpublished doctoral dissertation, University of Texas at Austin.

Baldwin, R. G. (2007). *Academic civility begins in the classroom.* Nederland, CO: The POD Network. Retrieved February 29, 2007, from http://cstl.syr.edu/CSTL3/Home/Resources/Subscriptions/POD/V9/V9N8.HTMl

Barber, B. R. (1998). *A place for us: How to make society civil and democracy strong.* New York: Hill and Wang.

Bloomfield College. (2007). *Statement on civility and human dignity.* Retrieved February 9, 2007, from www.bloomfield.edu/studentaffairs/civility2.asp

Caldwell, M. (1999). *A short history of rudeness: Manners, morals, and misbehavior in modern America.* New York: Picador.

Callahan, D., & Bok, S. (Eds.). (1980). *Ethics teaching in higher education.* New York: Plenum Press.

Carbone, E. (1999). Students behaving badly in large classes. In *New Directions in Teaching and Learning* (No. 77, pp. 35–43). San Francisco: Jossey-Bass.

Carter, S. L. (1998). *Civility: Manners, morals, and the etiquette of democracy.* New York: Basic Books.

Coe College. (2007). *Campus civility statement.* Retrieved February 9, 2007, from www.coe.edu/reslife/handbook/index.htm

Cohen, R. (2002). *The good, the bad, and the difference.* New York: Doubleday.

Dalton, J., & Watson, M. (1997). *Among friends: Classrooms where caring and learning prevail.* Oakland, CA: Developmental Studies Center.

Dechter, G. (2007, January 28). Class war. *The Baltimore Sun.*

Dewey, J. (1963). *Democracy and education.* New York: Macmillan. (Original work published 1916)

Dresser, N. (1996). *Multicultural manners: New rules of etiquette for a changing society.* New York: Wiley.

Eberly, D. E. (Ed.). (1994). *Building a community of citizens: Civil society in the 21st century.* Lanham, MD: University Press of America.

Eberly, D. E. (1998). *America's promise: Civil society and the renewal of American culture.* Lanham, MD: Rowman & Littlefield.

Etzioni, A. (1993). *The spirit of community: The reinvention of American society.* New York: Simon & Schuster.

Forni, P. M. (2002). *Twenty-five rules for considerate conduct.* New York: St. Martin's Press.

Gadamer, H.-G. (1988). *Truth and method.* New York: Crossroad.

Gilligan, C. (1982). *In a different voice.* Cambridge, MA: Harvard University Press.

Goldfarb, J. C. (1998). *Civility and subversion.* Cambridge, UK: Cambridge University Press.

Greenleaf, R. K. (1996). *On becoming a servant leader.* San Francisco: Jossey-Bass.

Gutmann, A. (1995). Civic education and social diversity. *Ethics: An International Journal of Social, Political and Legal Philosophy, 105(3),* 557–579.

Habermas, J. (1979). *Communication and the evolution of society* (T. McCarthy, Trans.). Boston: Beacon Press.

Hall, J. A. (Ed.). (1995). *Civil society: Theory, history, comparison.* Cambridge, UK: Polity Press.

Hardin, R. (1995). *One for all: The logic of group conflict.* Princeton, NJ: Princeton University Press.

Holladay, J. (2006). *Managing incivility in the college classroom* [Online article]. Austin: University of Texas. Retrieved February 9, 2007, from www.utexas.edu/academic/diia/gsi/tatalk/incivility.php

Hudson Valley Community College. (2007). *Civility, conduct, and respect at Hudson Valley Community College: What's expected of me?* [Workshop description]. Retrieved February 29, 2007, from https://www.hvcc.edu/civility/index.html

Jacobs, J. (1999, May 7). "Different" kids feel Littleton's backlash. *San Jose Mercury News,* p. B7.

Jamestown Community College. (2007). *Classroom civility guide for students.* Retrieved February 9, 2007, from www.sunyjcc.edu/college-wide/studentinfo/civilityguidestudents.htm

Keohane, N. (1996, November). *Moral education in the modern university.* Paper presented at the meeting of the American Philosophical Society, Philadelphia.

Kingwell, M. (1995). *A civil tongue: Justice, dialogue and the politics of pluralism.* University Park, PA: Pennsylvania State University Press.

Levine, A., & Cureton, J. S. (1998). *When hope and fear collide: A portrait of today's college student.* San Francisco: Jossey-Bass.

Long, E. L., Jr. (1992). *Higher education as a moral enterprise.* Washington, DC: Georgetown University Press.

Marks, J. (1996, April 22). The American uncivil wars. *U.S. News & World Report,* pp. 66–78.

McDill, E. (1998, March). *Civility in America today.* Paper presented at the Reassessing Civility Conference, Johns Hopkins University, Baltimore.

McEwen, B. C. (1997). Teaching diversity and civility: Part 2. *Instructional Strategies, 13*(2), 1–4.

McPartland, J. (1998, March). *Baltimore schools study.* Paper presented at the Reassessing Civility Conference, Johns Hopkins University, Baltimore.

National Center for Education Statistics. (2004). *Integrated Postsecondary Education Data System (IPEDS) fall enrollment survey* [Data file]. Washington, DC: U.S. Department of Education.

National Center for Education Statistics. (2005). National postsecondary student aid study, 2003–04 (NPSAS:04). Washington, DC: U.S. Department of Education.

National Education Association. Best practices: How to create classroom decorum by modeling it. In *Thriving in Academe* [Online forum]. Retrieved February 9, 2007, from www2.nea.org/he/advo00/advo0003/bestprac.html

Noddings, N. (1984). *Caring: A feminine approach to ethics and moral education.* Berkeley, CA: University of California Press.

Noddings, N. (1998, February). *A democratic approach to raising standards.* Paper presented at the Standards and Our Schools Conference, San Jose State University, CA.

Noddings, N. (2005a). Caring in education. In *The encyclopedia of informal education.* Retrieved February 29, 2007, from www.infed.org/biblio/noddings_caring_in_ education.htm

Noddings, N. (2005b). *The challenge to care in schools.* New York: Teachers College Press.

Pagden, A. (1998, March). *Cultures and civilities.* Paper presented at Reassessing Civility Conference, Johns Hopkins University, Baltimore.

Parker, W. C. (1997). The art of deliberation. *Educational Leadership, 54,* 18–21.

Penn National Commission on Society, Culture and Community. (2000). Key findings of the Penn National Commission. Retrieved February 29, 2007, from www.upenn.edu/pnc

Rachels, J. (1999). *The elements of moral philosophy* (3rd ed.). Boston: McGraw-Hill.

Rawls, J. (1972). *A theory of justice.* Cambridge, MA: Harvard University Press.

Reed, R. (2007). *Strategies for dealing with troublesome behaviors in the classroom.* National Teaching & Learning Forum. Retrieved February 29, 2007, from www.ntlf.com/html/pi/9710/strat.htm

Richardson, S. M. (Ed.). (1999). Promoting civility: A teaching challenge. In *New Directions in Teaching and Learning* (No. 77). San Francisco: Jossey-Bass.

Rodin, J. (1997, December 8). *The university and public behavior.* Paper presented at the meeting of the Penn National Commission on Society, Culture and Community, Washington, DC.

Rodin, J. (1998, July 30). Civilize public dialogue and shape a better world. *The Christian Science Monitor,* p. 11.

Rookstool, J. (2003). *Civility: Can it be taught in the classroom?* San Jose, CA: San Jose/ Evergreen Community College District, Teaching and Learning Center. For a copy of this document, go to www.sjeccd.org or contact Judy Rookstool at judy.rookstool@evc.edu

Rosen, B., & Caplan, A. C. (1980). *Ethics in the undergraduate curriculum.* Hastings, New York: The Hastings Center Institute of Society, Ethics and the Life Sciences.

Ryfe, D. (1998, December). *What is good discourse: A review of the literature.* Paper presented to the Penn National Commission on Society, Culture Plenary Meeting, Los Angeles.

Sacks, P. (1996). *Generation X Goes to College.* Chicago: Carus.

San Jose Community College. (1998). *SJCC campus climate study.* Unpublished document, San Jose Community College, CA.

Schneider, A. (1998, March 27). Insubordination and intimidation signal the end of decorum in many classrooms. *The Chronicle of Higher Education, 44*(29), 12–14.

Seligman, A. B. (1992). *The idea of civil society.* Princeton, NJ: Princeton University Press.

Singer, M. G. (Ed.). (1988). *American philosophy.* Cambridge: Cambridge University Press.

Sissa, G. (1998, March). *Graces and virtues: Timely questions on politeness.* Paper presented at the Reassessing Civility Conference, Johns Hopkins University, Baltimore.

Sorcinelli, M. D. (2003–2004). Encouraging civil behavior in large classes. *Essays on Teaching Excellence: Toward the Best in the Academy, 15*(8). Retrieved February 9, 2007, from http://oira.syr.edu/cstl2/Home/Teaching%20Support/Resources/ Subscriptions/POD/TE%20Vol%2015%20(03-04)/Encouraging%20Civil% 20Behavior%20in%20Large%20Classes.htm

StudentAffairs.com. (2007). *Promoting civility on campus* [Course outline]. Retrieved February 9, 2007, from www.studentaffairs.com/onlinecourses/winter2006 course8.html

Tiberius R. G., & Flack, E. (1999). Incivility in dydadic teaching and learning. In *New Directions in Teaching and Learning* (No. 77, pp. 3–12). San Francisco, CA: Jossey-Bass.

Town of Lexington. (2007). *Guidelines for civil discourse.* Retrieved February 9, 2007, from http://ci.lexington.ma.us/NoPlace4Hate/CivilDiscourse.htm

University of California, Davis. (2007). *The principles of community.* Retrieved February 9, 2007, from http://principles.ucdavis.edu

White, P. (1996). *Civic virtues and public schooling: Educating citizens for a democratic society.* New York: Teachers College Press.

Wiebe, R. (1998, December). *Report on primary tensions.* Paper presented at the plenary meeting of the Penn National Commission on Society, Culture and Community, Los Angeles.

Additional Resources

Print Resources

Alexander-Snow. (2004). Dynamics of gender, ethnicity, and race in understanding of classroom incivility. In *New Directions for Teaching and Learning* (No. 99, pp. 21–31). San Francisco: Jossey-Bass.

Amada, G. (1999). *Coping with misconduct in the college classroom: A practical model.* Asheville, NC: College Administration Publications.

Asmus, C. (2002). Cultivating civility. *Colorado State University Cooperative Extension and College of Applied Human Sciences Newsletter, 4*(2), 1–6.

Associated Press. (1999, 16 July). MBAs getting lessons in minding P's and Q's. *The Times Picayune.*

Axelrod, R. (1984). *The evolution of cooperation.* New York: Harper Collins.

Bayer, A. E. (2004). Promulgating statements of student rights and responsibilities. In *New Directions for Teaching and Learning* (No. 99, pp. 77–87). San Francisco: Jossey-Bass.

Bellah, R. N. (1986). *Habits of the heart: Individualism and commitment in American life.* New York: Harper and Row.

Bellah, R. N., Madsen, R., Sullivan, W., Swidler, A., & Tipton, S. (Eds.). (1987). *Individualism and commitment in American life: Readings on the themes of habits of the heart.* New York: Harper and Row.

Berger, Bruce A. (Ed.). (2002). *Promoting civility in pharmacy education.* Binghamton, NY: Haworth Press.

Boyer, E. (1990). *Campus life: In search of community.* San Francisco: The Carnegie Foundation for the Advancement of Teaching.

Braxton, J. M., & Bayer, A. E. (2004). Toward a code of conduct for undergraduate teaching. In *New Directions for Teaching and Learning* (No. 99, pp. 47–55). San Francisco: Jossey-Bass.

Bray, N. J., & Del Favero, M. (2004). Sociological explanations for faculty and student classroom incivilities. In *New Directions for Teaching and Learning* (No. 99, pp. 9–19). San Francisco: Jossey-Bass.

Bumphus, W. G. (1997). Mapping the road to reform and civility. *Community College Journal, 67*(5), 4.

Burgess, G., & Burgess, H. (1997). *The meaning of civility.* Boulder, CO: University of Colorado Conflict Research Consortium.

Bushman, R. L. (1996). The rise and fall of civility in America: The genteel republic. *The Wilson Quarterly*, Autumn, 14–23.

Cahn, S. M. (1995). *Classics of Western philosophy* (4th ed.). Indianapolis, IN: Hackett Publishing.

Cruz, A. M. (2001–2002). Civic responsibility, ethics and integrity. *Community College Journal, 72*(3), 33.

Douglass, M., & Friedmann, J. (Eds.). (1998). *Cities for citizens: Planning and the rise of civil society in a global age.* New York: Wiley.

Elias, N. (1978). *The civilizing process: Vol. 1. The history of manners* (E. Jephcott, Trans.). New York: Pantheon Books.

Elias, N. (1982). *The civilizing process: Vol. 2. Power and civility* (E. Jephcott, Trans.). New York: Pantheon Books.

Exley, R. (2003–2004). Morality across the curriculum. *Community College Journal, 74*(3), 11.

Exley, R. J., Gottlieb, K. L., & Young, J. B. (1999–2000). Citizenship and the community. *Community College Journal, 70*(3), 16.

Garcia, R. (2003–2004). Civic engagement: A pathway to service and learning. *Community College Journal, 74*(3), 14.

Gottlieb, K., & Robinson, G. (2003–2004). Integrating civic responsibility into the curriculum. *Community College Journal, 74*(3), 25.

Habermas, J. (1984). *The theory of communicative competence: Vol. 1. Reason and the rationalization of society* (T. McCarthy, Trans.). Boston: Beacon Press.

Heinemann, R. L. (1996, November). *Addressing campus-wide communication incivility in the basic course: A case study.* Paper presented at the annual meeting of the Speech Communication Association, San Diego, CA. (ERIC Document Reproduction Service No. ED 404 701).

Hirschy, A. S., & Braxton, J. M. (2004). Effects of student classroom incivilities on students. In *New Directions for Teaching and Learning* (No. 99, pp. 67–76). San Francisco: Jossey-Bass.

Hobbes, T. (1968). *Leviathan.* Harmondsworth, Middlesex, UK: Penguin. (Original work published 1651)

Johnson, S. (1999). An education in ethics. *Issues in Ethics, 10*(1).

Kasson, J. F. (1990). *Rudeness and civility: Manners in nineteenth century urban America.* New York: Hill and Wang.

Kauffman, J. M., & Burbach, H. J. (1998). Creating classroom civility. *Education Digest, 63*, 13–18.

Kohlberg, L. (1981). *The philosophy of moral development.* San Francisco: Harper and Row.

Law would require courtesy at school. (1999, June 18). *San Jose Mercury News*, p. A4.

Lisman, C. D. (1999–2000). Ethics in the curriculum. *Community College Journal, 70*(3), 36.

Martin, J. (1996). *Miss Manners rescues civilization: From sexual harassment, frivolous lawsuits, dissing, and other lapses in civility.* New York: Crown.

Martin, J. (1998, March). *Civility.* Paper presented at the Reassessing Civility Conference, Johns Hopkins University, Baltimore.

Martin, J. (1999, May 15). What parents can teach their kids. *San Jose Mercury News,* p. C8.

Martin, J., & Gunther, S. S. (1990). I think: Therefore I thank. A philosophy of etiquette. *American Scholar, 59,* 237–255.

May, L., Collins-Chobanian, S., & Wong, K. (Eds.). (1998). *Applied ethics: A multicultural approach.* Upper Saddle River, NJ: Prentice Hall.

McDonald, W. . & Associates. (2002). *Creating campus community: In search of Ernest Boyer's legacy.* San Francisco: Jossey-Bass.

Mill, J. S. (1956). *On liberty.* Indianapolis, IN: Bobbs-Merrill Co.

Morris, J. (1996). The rise and fall of civility in America: Democracy beguiled. *The Wilson Quarterly, Autumn,* 24–35.

Putnam, R. D. (1995). Bowling alone: America's declining social capital. *Journal of Democracy, 6,* 65–78.

Q & A with David Pierce: What is institutional citizenship. (2000). *Community College Journal, 70*(5), 55.

Sanchez, R. (1997, January 13). Survey of college freshmen finds rise in volunteerism. *The Washington Post,* p. A1.

Schneewind, J. (1998, March). *Distinguishing norms.* Paper presented at the Reassessing Civility Conference, Johns Hopkins University, Baltimore.

Schwinn, C., & Schwinn, D. (2000). A call to community: The CC role in comprehensive community development. *Community College Journal, 70*(5), 24.

Selzer, S. M. (2000). *By George: Mr. Washington's guide to civility today.* Kansas City, MO: Andrews McMeel.

Sorcinelli, M. D. (2002). Promoting civility in large classes. In C. A. Stanley & M. E. Porter (Eds.), *Engaging large classes* (pp. 44–57). Bolton, MA: Anker.

Spears, L. C. (Ed.). (1995). *Reflections on leadership.* New York: Wiley.

Strenski, I. (1993, June 23). Recapturing the values that promote civility on the campuses. *Chronicle of Higher Education,* p. A36.

Strike, K., & Moss, P. A. (1997). *Ethics and college student life.* Boston: Allyn and Bacon.

Walters, R. (1998, March). *Civility in America today.* Paper presented at the Reassessing Civility Conference, Johns Hopkins University, Baltimore.

Woolford-Singh, A. (2000). Race: Creating a campus dialogue. *Community College Journal, 70*(5), 52.

Youniss, J., McLellan, J. A., & Yates, M. (1997). What we know about engendering civic identity. *American Behavioral Scientist, 40,* 620–672.

Online Resources

Web Sites

Colorado State University Family and Youth Institute
www.cahs.colostate.edu/fyi

Johns Hopkins University Civility Project
www.jhu.edu/civility

Nova Southeastern University Civility Project
http://shss.nova.edu/civility

Penn National Commission on Society, Culture and Community
www.upenn.edu/pnc

Penn State University Janet Neff Sample Center for Manners and Civility
www.pserie.psu.edu/academic/hss/samplecenter

University of Colorado Conflict Research Consortium
www.colorado.edu/conflict/civility.htm

Wingspread—The Johnson Foundation
www.johnsonfdn.org

Civility Statements/Codes

California State University at Pomona
www.csupomona.edu/~faculty_center/learning_links/index.htm

Ocean County College (NJ)
www.ocean.edu/campus/PAR/civility.htm

Alfred State University (SUNY)
www.alfredstate.edu/alfred/Student_Conduct_Code.asp

MiraCosta College (CA)
www.miracosta.cc.ca.us/home/kcunningham/AcademicStandards.pdf

Civility Courses

Blinn College (TX)
"Classroom Civility: Managing Bothersome to Belligerent Behaviors"
http://sacs.blinn.edu/Classroom civility/index.htm

Colgate University (NY)
"Promoting Civility on Campus"
www.studentaffairs.com/onlinecourses/winter2006course8.html

New York College Learning Skills Association
"Improving Civility in the College Classroom and Learning Center"
www.nyclsa.org/conference_schedule.htm#icc

Online Documents

"Civility in the Classroom: Tips for Dealing With Troublesome Behavior"—
Texas Tech University
www.depts.ttu.edu/studentaffairs/publications/civility2002.pdf

"Have College Professors Lost Control of Their Classrooms? A Look at Classroom Civility
in the New Millennium. Is Rudeness on the Rise in College Classrooms?"—Troy Lepper
www.missouri.edu/~petwww/library/chalkboard/fall2000/rudeness.htm

"Helping Different Types of Distressed Students"—University of California-Santa
Barbara Counseling & Career Services and the Office of Office of Instructional
Consultation
http://id-www.ucsb.edu/ic/ta/hdbk/ta6-3.html

"Lessons in civility"—Michael Berube
http://chronicle.com/free/v50/i15/15b00701.htm

"Managing Hot Moments in the Classroom"—Lee Warren
http://teaching.concordia.ca/docs/Bok_HotMoments.pdf

"The Meaning of Civility"—Guy Burgess and Heidi Burgess
www.colorado.edu/conflict/civility.htm

"Reducing Incivility in the University/College Classroom"—Patrick J. Morrissette
www.ucalgary.ca/%7Eiejll/volume5/morrissette.html

"Short Pieces on Civility in the College Classroom"—Steven Richardson
www.nea.org/he/advo00/advo0003/thriving.html

"When Our Students Don't Respect Us"—Thomas H. Benton
http://chronicle.com/jobs/2004/01/2004010501c.htm

Index

academic leaders and civility theory, 13–16

Anscombe, G. E. M., 4

Aquinas, Thomas, 5

Aristotle, 1, 5–6

Barber, Benjamin, 8, 11

biology curriculum, ethics in, 25

Bloomfield College, 49–50

Bok, S., 24, 26, 27

Caldwell, M., 12–13

Callahan, D., 24, 26, 27

campus, promoting civility on, 42

campus activities, incorporate civility into, 26–27

campus-related recommendations, 39

Caplan, A. C., 24

Carter, Stephen L., 6

categorical imperative, 4

character education, 1

citizenship, importance of, 19–20

citizenship and civil discourse, toward, 10–11.

   See also discourse mutual respect, 12–13

civic education, obstacles to providing, 15

Civic Purpose Committee, 21

civic virtue, 5–7, 10

Civic Virtues and Public Schooling (White), 30–31

civil conversation, 10–11

civil discourse. *See* citizenship and civil discourse; discourse

civil state/civil society, 5, 10, 11

civil state theory, 8–9

civil talk, 11

About the Author

Judy Rookstool has filled a number of positions within the San Jose/Evergreen Community College (SJECC) District. For much of her career as an academic and personal counselor, Rookstool was responsible for assisting students with goal setting, career choice, academic program planning, and personal adjustments. In addition, she has taught developmental English and student guidance. As director of school and community relations, Rookstool developed and implemented programs in community relations, high school outreach, alumni association, and college advancement. As director of student activities she was responsible for associated student activities, including academic, social, and cultural events. She oversaw student participation in college governance and instructed a student leadership course.

Rookstool used the opportunity of a sabbatical leave to develop a body of knowledge on civility in the classroom, a subject she has promoted in various presentations. She also received a SJECC District Carnegie Scholar Award, completing a classroom action research project on teaching civility in the classroom in 2002. Before beginning in education, Rookstool worked at a community action agency, co-directing a summer readiness program emphasizing career guidance for economically disadvantaged students, as a career counselor and as a program evaluator.

Rookstool received a BA (with honors) in sociology from the University of California, Santa Barbara, an MA (with honors) in counselor education from San Jose State University, and an EdD in organization and leadership from the University of San Francisco. Currently she is the coordinator of the Teaching and Learning Center at Evergreen Valley College—a center to support faculty and staff professional development.